THE PURPOSE BEHIND THE PROBLEM

*The Purpose Behind
The Problem*

By

Margie Hoskins

THE PURPOSE BEHIND THE PROBLEM

©The Purpose Behind The Problem
Copyright© MARGIE HOSKINS
First edition 2021
ISBN: 978-0-620-84067-5
All rights reserved
This book or any parts thereof may not be reproduced in any form, Stored in a retrieval system or transmitted in any form by any Means electronically, mechanical, photocopy, recording or otherwise – Without prior written permission of the Author: Margie Hoskins and Chillidave Publishers.
Contacts: (071) 441 9020
(081) 805 8054
Chillidave30@gmail.com
chillidavepublishers@gmail.com
Cover design by: Tlhompho David
Edited by: Chillidave Publishers
Published by: Chillidave Publishers

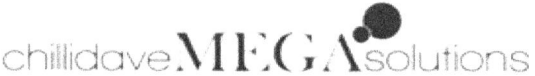

THE PURPOSE BEHIND THE PROBLEM

Dedication

To Joshua Project for allowing me to use all the resources for completing this book and to Becky Vaughan, who was the 'angel' that God had sent, not only to edit my book but to be there for me when God had placed me on a rocky road, and I needed someone to hold my hand.
And most of all to the body of Christ the Lord Jesus for His guidance and inspiration to complete this book.

THE PURPOSE BEHIND THE PROBLEM

Foreword

The warmth of the Lord's powerful, majestic presence engulfed me I sat in my bedroom. I could not stop crying. It was a warm autumn afternoon; the wind caused some dry leaves to do the swirly dance just outside my bedroom window. I stared at the painting hanging on the opposite wall of my room. The colors seemed to blur under my tears. I reached for a tissue and blew my nose, my mind recalling everything that had just happened.

I still could not believe it and had to pinch myself amid the tears to make sure I was not dreaming.

The Lord had led me to leave my hometown in Kwazulu-Natal and head to the Eastern Cape, with no job, no furniture but my suitcase of clothes, with no idea how I was going to survive.

Years later, the Lord spoke to me about writing this book. I had just returned home from our usual Sunday Morning Worship service, had my lunch and decided to have an afternoon nap. I was exhausted from my busy schedule from a few days before.

So when I woke up that Sunday afternoon, refreshed from my nap but still inspired from God's Word, I decided to have a cup of tea. Singing my favorite hymn, I made my way to the kitchen. I then felt the sudden urge to be alone so I left my husband, Enver and my son, Tyrell, watching television and slowly made my way

THE PURPOSE BEHIND THE PROBLEM

back to my bedroom. I immediately became aware of a loving, warm, divine and majestic presence and I knew it was the presence of God. Forgetting about my tea, I surrendered to the Lord as He rained down His presence and I began to weep and to submit to Him. I lifted my hands and felt as if I was swept away to a place filled with angels, worshipping the Almighty God. I heard God's still yet powerful voice saying "Margie my daughter, I want you to start writing the book you always wanted to write, I am going to guide you as you write. I want you to know that it is time now and after this book is written, you will never be the same again."

The tears just flowed, as I sat and wept in the Lord's presence, absorbing what I had heard with so much gratitude.
 I did not even know where I would begin, but I believed if the Lord said so, then it would be so. I did not know *when* and I did not know *how* but I believed God would make it possible.
My mind flashed back to my life's experiences that I had written down since I had given my heart to the Lord. I had been writing my life story and had no idea why. Now I began to understand that it was not in vain. God always has a reason when we do things without us knowing why.

Wiping the tears from my eyes, I prayed this prayer "Father, I have never written a book before but I want to be obedient to you. Please dear Lord, bring people into my life that would understand and help me. Amen."

THE PURPOSE BEHIND THE PROBLEM

Immediately the name Rebecca Vaughan popped into my mind. I had met her at a Community Workers workshop when I had attended the course. Becky, as she was known, was a very powerful and dynamic woman of God who had written her own manual. I thanked the Lord, this was my start. I knew I had to set up a meeting to meet with Becky.

After spending a few days in prayer, I sent Becky a message asking if we could meet and Becky agreed that we could meet at work the following day probably after two o' clock. I was overjoyed and thanked God.
To my amazement, Becky walked into my office around 1:10pm the next day. We greeted each other with an affectionate hug and after that it was straight down to business. I got straight to the point. I told Becky how the Lord had spoken to me about writing this book and how her name had popped into my mind when I had prayed. The next few minutes I could feel the tears pricking at the back of my eyes as Becky shared her experience. Her testimony was similar to mine…coming Jeffrey's Bay also with no job, no furniture, and no idea how she was going to survive. She at least had a bike which I did not even have.

Tears splashed down my cheeks as Becky shared what the Lord had shown her…. God was going to use me as a motivational speaker and the Lord was going to use this book to open doors in my life and to bring glory and honor to His Name.

THE PURPOSE BEHIND THE PROBLEM

I immediately realized God never makes mistakes; Becky and I were already connected in Spirit.
More tears followed as Becky shared some of the things which I had already experienced, incidents which God was revealing to her, which she did not even know about. God was already at work. This was no co-incidence; this was God's plan to connect us. In that brief visit, God had already used Becky to inspire me and even before she left, we joined hands in prayer as we dedicated myself and this book to the Almighty and Powerful God. We prayed that His plan and His purpose for this book would be accomplished not by what I had written, not by my experiences, but by the anointing that is on this book from the Lord Jesus Himself.

God richly bless you as you journey through this book on the powerful wings of the Holy Spirit…...

THE PURPOSE BEHIND THE PROBLEM

Table of Contents

Dedication
....Page 2

Foreword
....Page 3

Shattered and Broken
....Page 9

Let your Will be done in my Life
....Page 13

Vision and Provision
....Page 17

I know the Plans for You
....Page 21

A New Creation in Christ
....Page 28

Repaid for what the Locusts have eaten
....Page 36

Heaven or Hell
....Page 40

THE PURPOSE BEHIND THE PROBLEM

Transformed by Trouble
....Page 45

Surrender and Obedience
....Page 50

I have plans for you, Arise
....Page 55

I know the Plans I have for You
....Page 64

Fear versus Faith
....Page 70

Warning and Breakthrough
....Page 73

It never Rains but Pours
....Page 77

Noah's Ark
....Page 81

Pain, Heartache and Tears to release the Past
....Page 84

Look at the Purpose and not the Problem
....Page 87

THE PURPOSE BEHIND THE PROBLEM

Reference
....Page 94

Acknowledgments
....Page 96

For Bookings
....Page 97

Authors Profile
....Page 98

THE PURPOSE BEHIND THE PROBLEM

CHAPTER 1

Shattered and Broken

It was a beautiful warm day.
I unlocked the office as usual that Thursday morning, deactivated the alarm, switched on the computer and neatened my desk. I made sure that the invoice book, stapling machine together with everything else I needed for the day, was neatly arranged on the desk before I rushed off to pray. I always prayed before the staff or the clients arrived, dedicating my day to the Lord and dedicating the business to God.

I enjoyed my job as an office clerk, joking with the clients who came in to pay their life insurance or funeral policies. I loved sharing the Gospel with those who had lost their loved ones and encouraged them with the scriptures from God's Word. I knew the pain of losing a loved one as I had lost three siblings as well as my parents.

On days that the office was not so busy, I had the opportunity to complete my Bible studies. When clients walked in and they saw the open Bible, they would ask questions and this gave me an opportunity to share about Jesus and the free gift of salvation. I was not ashamed to talk about the Lord. My colleagues knew I was born again and as their supervisor, I was an inspiration and led by example. God had given me the best job; I could study and minister His Word at all times. My brothers and sisters in Christ, from our church, Antioch Assembly

THE PURPOSE BEHIND THE PROBLEM

would pop in and we had wonderful times sharing about the goodness of God.

That afternoon, at 16:35pm I received a call from our Head Office. Mr. Gama told me that my contract had been terminated and that someone was on their way with the forms for me to sign.
"Financial problems……" his voice trailed off and cut the call before I could ask further questions. I was furious. I knew this was not true, the company was doing well financially and better still since I had been praying in the office every morning. Fortunately, I was alone in the office that afternoon. My assistant, Cindy had already left and our driver was elsewhere on a call out. I had the chance to consult with God after the call and realized it had to be a mistake. God knew how faithful I was to Him and to my bosses at Head Office. They had after all entrusted me to run this branch and I did so without any problems. No, it was definitely a misunderstanding and my contract was valid for another two years. I stared through the big glass windows at the entrance to the office, trying to figure out what the problem was. The afternoon sun blinked brightly in the sky and caused the letters printed on the glass, to cast patterns on the tiled floor. I had signed up so many new clients. Luke, the manager from the Pietermaritzburg branch was so impressed with my performance. I still remembered his words "Mrs. Hoskins you have enlarged our client base; you are a God-send."

When Mr. Andrews arrived, he was very rude and impatient and I was left with no choice but to sign the

THE PURPOSE BEHIND THE PROBLEM

form. When I had signed, he rushed off, refusing to answer my questions. When I tried to phone Head Office, the phone just rang and rang and no one answered.

I felt like my whole life was shattered after those few minutes. How could this be? "Lord, how could you let this happen?" I asked God. Part of me could not believe what had just happened. I felt so hurt and confused. I could feel the tears pricking at the back of my eyes. "What have I done wrong, how am I going to cope financially without a job?" I began to angrily clear my desk.

"Why, why me Lord?" I asked God feeling so betrayed as anger began to swell up inside of me. I felt that God had let me down, that He could have prevented me from losing my job. I mean He is God and nothing is impossible for Him. I wanted answers from Him. He knew my heart; He knew me…but He said nothing!

I wondered how God could let this happen when I ministered His word every day in the office to family, friends and clients, when I prayed here every single day and studied His word without being ashamed to speak about Him, when……the telephone rang and prevented me from hitting my fists on the desk. I was so hurt and angry. I felt that God had abandoned me.

Candice Hammond, my cousin from Jeffrey's Bay, could not believe what had happened. She knew something was wrong the minute I had answered the phone.

"Why would God take your job away if you have done nothing wrong?" Neither of us could understand.

Candice had previously begged me to visit her for the June holidays but I had always made excuses that my job

THE PURPOSE BEHIND THE PROBLEM

kept me too busy. Now that my job had come to an end, she persuaded me that it was the right time to visit her. She was even prepared to make the bus booking for me but going to Jeffrey's Bay was the last thing on my mind at that moment. I replaced the receiver, took one last look around and wiping the last tear, took my belongings and went home.

THE PURPOSE BEHIND THE PROBLEM

CHAPTER 2

Your Will Be Done

My best friend and prayer partner, Alfreda Hargreaves shared my pain and encouraged me after a few days "Do not worry God will open up another door for you, just trust Him."
But I felt that I would never get another job like my previous one. I really loved that job and enjoyed what I did. I could read and study God's Word and encourage His people…. but now it was gone.
 Freda committed herself to visiting me each day and the more we shared about Jesus, the more we grew and matured spiritually. Other times we spent time in prayer and watched inspiring DVDs. We completed a series of eight teachings of *David Asscherick's*[1] and this really impacted my life positively. God also touched my life through the study on closed doors and open doors.[2]

A slammed door has a harsh sound and is even harder to experience especially when we are seeking God's will. God closes doors in our lives not necessarily because we are living in sin, sometimes it's in the will of God. A closed door sometimes brings pain and heartache but through this God is taking us into a better job or situation or shaping us into the image of His Son. Revelation 3 tells us God holds the key, He can shut and open doors in our lives at any time. The door He shuts, no man can

THE PURPOSE BEHIND THE PROBLEM

open and the door He opens, no man can shut because He has the authority. God also has the right to slam doors without explanation. Sometimes when a door of opportunity is shut, it is to lead us through a better door with greater opportunities. Sometimes we cannot accept the closed door and we get a crowbar to force it open not realizing God has the key. Anytime we force open a closed door thinking we will get our way we will regret it at a later stage. We must leave it closed, back away and accept it. In acceptance lies peace! Sometimes we are so determined that this is what we're supposed to be doing that it is hard to accept that the door is truly closed. It is easy to be disillusioned and discouraged and think we have missed God's will, when we in fact are in the very nucleus of that will.

When doors are shut or opened, our lives have to change. My life definitely changed

God had planned that I watch this DVD on the right day and at the right time when I was angry and upset, when I felt that God was unfair, when I felt that God was punishing me for something that I had not done. But after a few days I began to understand that when we go through trials, tests, problems and heartache, it is not God punishing us as we always think, but it's God preparing us for our calling. Sometimes we see the preparation process as 'punishment from God because we have done something 'wrong' as in my case. When we are part of God's family, then we become part of His pre-determined or determined Will[3] meaning God has a

THE PURPOSE BEHIND THE PROBLEM

plan worked out for us even before we were born as He says in Jeremiah 11:4 that *before I formed you in the womb I knew you, before you were born I set you apart.*

The more I connected with God, the more the disappointments and discouragement began to fade from my life. I began to understand that God had a reason for every challenge that I had faced whether happy and blessed or disappointed and sorrowful. God loves me so much that he cares about the tiniest incident in my life and nothing escapes His notice. God has a purpose behind every problem. God is in charge of what happens, when it happens, why it happens and even what happens after it happens. A picture of me in the office flashed before my eyes and I could see how angry, how hurt, confused and disappointed I was. I even questioned God and cried for days. If only I understood, then what I knew now. I went on my knees and repented for being angry and bitter at God. I now had a better understanding as to why God had closed the door to my job. Romans 8:28 came to mind *all things work together for good to those who love God, to those who are called according to His purpose.*

My eyes were no longer on my problem but on the Lord. This helped me to grow spiritually. Candice would not give up and insisted that I leave home and go to Jeffrey's Bay and this got me thinking. I began to pray and fast about it. Freda and I got down to some serious fasting and prayer for the whole month of October. God was faithful to His word in Philippians 4:19 *and supplied all*

THE PURPOSE BEHIND THE PROBLEM

my needs according to His riches in glory through Christ Jesus.
Daily my faith and my strength in the Lord increased as He met my needs and I just rejoiced even though I had no idea of how I was going to survive for the next few months. All I could do was to rely on God and believe His promise in Ephesians 1:11 which states *because God has chosen me in advance He had a plan worked out for me and* I believed this with all my heart.

THE PURPOSE BEHIND THE PROBLEM

CHAPTER 3

Vision and Provision

I had just switched the kettle on after my morning prayer when the phone rang. It was Candice, "Listen Marg, don't worry about money, I am going to book your tickets so all you have to do is get on the bus and come down."
Candice made it sound so easy. I put my cell phone down and flopped into my favorite chair, my mind went back to the dream I had the night before. Could this be the answer?
Could it really be that the Lord wanted me to go to Jeffrey's Bay? That's like going to a totally different province never mind a new city!
I did not want to doubt God so I spent time waiting on God for confirmation. What I knew was that if this was God then everything would fall into place, even if I did not have a cent to my name. God does not work with money but with lives and hearts. God is never interested in how much money we have in the bank, as long as we are on His mandate, He will get us to where He wants us to be. We just need to allow God to do what He needs to do and co-operate.

A few days later, the Lord did give us the answer and although Freda was not happy about me leaving, she soon realized that this was God's plan. We were going to miss each other like crazy. We were friends since

THE PURPOSE BEHIND THE PROBLEM

Primary School. Candice phoned to say that our tickets had been booked for the 5th December.
"But Candice, the school closes on that day" I complained.
"So? You can fetch the kids and their reports once you are done with your packing. Oh, and do not forget the school transfers" she reminded me.
 There was my answer!
I finally had to accept that I was leaving. It suddenly felt weird going to a strange place and going to live there but I suddenly felt the assurance from the Lord that He will take care of me because He is taking me there. It is His plan for my life.

Three days before I could leave, I put up posters to sell my furniture. I once again asked the Lord "Father if it is your will for me to sell everything, let it be so." I will have to start over when I get to Jeffrey's Bay. On my way home, I received the first call. Someone wanted to buy my television set, someone else wanted to know if the refrigerator had already been sold so the calls and the sales went on and by that afternoon, most of my stuff had already been sold.

The day before I could leave, the Lord filled me with such excitement; I began to thank God daily that His Will would be accomplished in my life. My husband was not too enthusiastic about leaving, he thought I had gone crazy, but I knew he would come around once he realized that this was part of God's plan, that we were on His mandate. Crazy as it sounded, I knew deep down in my heart that I was at peace about leaving, that I was not

THE PURPOSE BEHIND THE PROBLEM

making a mistake and that I had fasted and spent time in prayer waiting upon God to make sure that it was not me, but God who wanted me to go to Jeffrey's Bay. Even my son Cameron who was fourteen and his younger brother, Tyrell who was eight, was so excited. My Pastor also realized that I was serious about leaving when he heard that all my furniture was sold.

On the 5th of December, when I boarded the bus, I knew this was it; there was no turning back. Tears were followed by tight hugs, as we said our goodbyes to friends and family. Once aboard, I asked the Lord to close the door to my past, that I would never go back unless the Lord sends me back home and that no matter what challenges I would face on my new encounter, that His grace would be sufficient for me. I was not even going into a job; I had no idea how I was going to make it. All I knew was that I believed in the Sovereignty of God, meaning the all-wise, all-knowing God rules and reigns in realms beyond my comprehension to bring about a stop to His plan for my life. His plan included all promotions, adversity and prosperity, financial challenges, tragedy and calamity sadness and joy, illness and health, perilous times and comfort, safety, prosperity and ease.

I believed that God would never leave me nor forsake me.

And as the saying goes '*Those who know their God, knows that He knows, even when they do not know….* So instead of giving up or giving in, they give thanks!

THE PURPOSE BEHIND THE PROBLEM

I was ready to let God accomplish that which He had planned and purposed for me. I once again remembered the prophetic words that were spoken over me and my prayer was "Lord, let your will be done in my life and let every single prophecy come to pass as I start a new life in a new place with you."

THE PURPOSE BEHIND THE PROBLEM

CHAPTER 4

I Know the Plans I have for you

The evening sky had dulled as night set in. The lights from every little town that we passed along the way looked like millions of stars, flickering against the darkened sky. As I sat in the bus pondering how everything had happened, I began to offer a silent prayer to God. I now realized why my contract had ended *His ways are not our ways*, as His word states. He had other plans for me.
I also realized that because God is sovereign and in full control, He would take full responsibility for my results that I need not try to carry the burden. It was not up to me to make the divine plan work; it was up to God. My job was to continue to walk in His will. God promised me in Isaiah 58:9 *that when I call, He will answer. When I cry out for help, then he will say here am I.* I believed and knew that God would answer my cry for help. Going to start over in a new place was not going to be easy but I knew God was at work through my disappointments and broken dreams. It was hard to have my dreams dashed of not staying in my hometown with my family and friends. To face a future that was unknown and unfamiliar was scary but God knew the plans He had for me. He was just guiding me onto the right path and in the right direction. I knew I could trust God with my life.

Suddenly it was if the mist had cleared and I began to understand as the Holy Spirit began to minister to me -

THE PURPOSE BEHIND THE PROBLEM

the fasting, the studying of God's Word, the challenges, every trial, test and problem with my family, my husband, friends and colleagues…. was preparation. This was God's way of preparing me for where He was taking me.

My mind flashed back to some of the experiences, challenges and incidents that I had now faced up to. My experience with the Outreach Team; I will never forget how this changed my life. Our group used to go to the Chest Hospital every Sunday afternoon to pray with the patients who were HIV positive, who were severely sick with cancer, tuberculosis and other sicknesses. Some of these patients had given up hope of living because they were too sick. The group would pray for them and share God's Word with them. This became a weekly routine since the patients looked forward to our group coming each week. We would begin in the children's ward and dance and sing Sunday school songs with the little ones and give them coloring books and a little snack before moving to the other wards.
But one particular day as the team was ready to leave; there was this little child in the cot that caught my attention. I touched his little hand and felt the strong urge to pray for him. He was HIV positive and very thin. I could see his rib-cage and the rise and fall of his tiny little body as he struggled to breathe. For the first time I felt a wave of compassion fill my life. I looked at him and the tears just filled my eyes. I felt heart-sore to see a baby suffer. He must have been two years old but he looked so small.

THE PURPOSE BEHIND THE PROBLEM

For weeks these pictures stayed in my mind after leaving the hospital. Flashes of grown-up men and women in napkins, too weak and sick to help themselves. Men and women on beds with their ribcages showing through their flesh from lack of appetite, too sick to eat, with sunken in eyes and hollow cheeks, death knocking at their door.
The Outreach group would go to each and every bed and pray, trusting God and leading each willing patient to accept the Lord into their lives. When we returned each week, we would find empty beds as patients had passed on to be with the Lord. Sometimes we would be surprised by patients who would be healed and able to walk. They would then share their testimony on our next visit.

God made me realize that seeing sick people in a movie or on television and being moved is not as emotional and hurting as seeing them before your very eyes. For in reality, the Lord is able to make us aware that the person needs prayer, that the person is dying and needs Jesus otherwise they are going to a lost eternity (hell) if they have not accepted Jesus into their life. God was also able to let me feel empathy for the suffering and the sick. I remember the many time I held back my tears to see people lying there sick and helpless, about to give up on life, with no strength to fight. But God's Word tells us that *we will lay hands on the sick and they shall recover through the healing power and the blood of Jesus.* It is the same powerful, anointed blood of Jesus that is able to heal the sick hence God's word in Isaiah 53:5 *he was pierced for our transgressions. He was crushed for our*

THE PURPOSE BEHIND THE PROBLEM

iniquities, the punishment that brought us peace was upon Him and by his stripes we are healed.
 God was teaching me that His blood was able to heal all diseases and sicknesses. I am forever grateful that the Lord had blessed me with good health. I know I was forever indebted to Jesus and could never repay Him for dying on the cross for me. It cost Christ much to shed his blood for my sins. It is the same anointed blood that sets the captives free.

I sat on the bus with tears in my eyes as the Lord reminded me of this experience. God did not stop there. He reminded me of the day of spiritual battle against demonic forces.
I will never forget that day. It was a Sunday afternoon, I had just returned home after being with the Outreach Team, when my brother and his family came over to our house. Unaware of what awaited me; I walked into the kitchen and made myself a cup of tea. My brother approached me "I want you to find a place and move out!" I told him okay, I will move out as soon as I had found a place but he followed me to my room, his tone of voice louder and harsh than before "Listen here I want you to find a place, to move out of here." I repeated what I had told him the first time but he kept on following me up and down the passage, swearing me. I immediately sensed something was wrong and tried to get away from him to pray. He continued to swear at me and insult me and the feeling to pray became stronger. I walked down the passage to the lounge. Our house had a sunken in lounge and he followed, swearing all the time. He stood on the steps and swore while I walked round and around

THE PURPOSE BEHIND THE PROBLEM

the coffee table calling on the Name of Jesus, binding and canceling the plans of the enemy and praying against every demonic power and evil spirit. The more I prayed, the louder he shouted, the more I rebuked the enemy, the more vulgar he became.

I took my tea, walked back to my room but he tried to get a hold of me and I pulled away, sensing that I had to continue praying to allow God to take over. I began to pray with authority in Jesus Name and felt the warmth of God's presence in the room. I began to do spiritual warfare, binding and canceling the plan of the enemy to destroy me. I saw evil in my brother's eyes as he came toward me and I felt the anointed power of God beginning to swell up inside of me and I began to jump up and down like a bouncing ball. I suddenly felt hot, as if burning coals of fire was thrown on me- Holy Ghost fire and I began to pray in tongues.

I do not know what had happened in those few seconds but when I opened my eyes, the house was empty and silent. My brother and his family were gone. I did not even hear the car so I do not know when they had left. I was filled with such peace. I took my cold cup of tea and warmed it in the microwave.

Later that evening, my kids and I held hands and prayed before they got into bed, thanking the Lord that His power is stronger than any other. We got into bed and I wondered how my brother was feeling. I wanted to phone him but my cell phone battery was flat. While Cameron put my phone on charge, the Lord urged me to read Psalm 91. I sat in bed and read it aloud as my kids

THE PURPOSE BEHIND THE PROBLEM

fell asleep. Suddenly I heard a knock at the door and I saw a hand signaling to me to "come" It was my brother. I froze in shock. He signaled to me to go outside, led me through the front door, out the gate to his car. I was suddenly gripped with fear but the Lord assured me that He was with me and that I was safe. I got into the car and he drove to his house looking very worried and troubled. The minute we reached his house, his wife ran out, opened the car door and started confessing. She said it was the first time she had heard her husband swearing the way he did, that she could not handle it and blocked her ears. She felt so ashamed and apologized for his terrible behavior. I told her that it was not his fault but she continued by saying "My husband was so troubled since he came home and he knew he won't be able to sleep. He just felt that he had to come to you and apologize and he knew it was the Lord."

Then my brother finally spoke "I had no right to say what I did to you, you are my sister and I don't know why I said all those nasty and terrible things, I am sorry" I forgave him and explained that I understood it was not him but an evil curse of witchcraft and that God had already taken care of whatever it was sent to do. I also explained to him that just before he could open my bedroom door, I was reading Psalm 91, which is a prayer of protection, and that God's mighty hand of protection was already covering the family.

That night as I stepped back into the house, I could not stop thanking God; tears of joy were just rolling down my cheeks. I felt so close to God I could feel His love burning in my heart and in my soul and He had proved

THE PURPOSE BEHIND THE PROBLEM

that in troubled times, all I had to do was to listen and obey. I thanked Him for my victory.

All this had been God's plan of preparation. I wiped away the tears, looking around in the bus to see if anyone noticed my tears but everyone was occupied by their own thoughts so I just allowed the Lord to have his way. The Holy Spirit then began to minister to me and made me realize that life, especially the Christian walk is a big test. Only when we pass the test or the trial or the challenge; then God is able to reward us with a blessing. I was no longer afraid; in fact, I was now more anxious to get to Jeffrey's Bay because I knew that not every challenge, problem and test that I had to face was in vain. God had prepared me throughout my Christian walk. Suddenly the weird feeling vanished- I felt I was not alone; God was with me every step of the way. God knew the only way to get my attention was to close the door to my job, it had nothing to do with what I had done or did not do, and it was God's perfect timing for His perfect plan.

I thought back to my response when Candice had invited me to Jeffrey's Bay, the many times I had refused, but God knew what His plans were for me and He had actually used Candice to carry out His plan and accomplished His will for my life- no wonder she never gave up!
Sometimes when we are faced with a challenge or a problem, the last thing we want to remember is that God is using the very same problem to empower us for the future.

THE PURPOSE BEHIND THE PROBLEM

CHAPTER 5

A New creation in Christ

Although God protects us in a wonderful way without us realizing it, He allows us now and again to experience His protecting grace in a more visible way.

I grew up as the eldest daughter of a large family of nine children. After I was born, I had to stay in hospital for three weeks because of health complications. My mom told me years later that she had almost 'lost' me but the Lord Jesus had reasons for keeping me alive. When I got older, I had epileptic fits and the seizures got so bad that my parents would force a teaspoon into my mouth to keep my jaws from locking. It seems Satan had tried to destroy me from birth but failed. During my earliest childhood in Richmond, I had followed my brothers to the river when they went for a swim and accidently fell into the deep water. God saved my life by allowing one of my brothers to rescue me on time. A few years later when the family went on an outing to Howick Falls, I was learning to swim, the current pushed me to the deep end where the water covered my head. God again saved my life. When I was in the dance club years later, a fight broke out and a chair was flung in the air, which missed my head, just by inches. On another occasion, I almost drowned together with my three sisters on New Year's Day on a family outing.

When I got married many years later, my husband was with my brother at the Sports Bar. They were discussing

whether to participate in the darts competition that was to be held later that day. Enver had asked me to wait with them for a few minutes but I just had the urge to go home. It was without doubt the Hand of God that caused my two-year-old son to become hungry and restless, leaving Enver and I with no choice but to go home. A few hours later, we heard that there had been a shootout at the very same place. Eight people had been bloodily massacred including my brother.
The same God has again and again protected me in numerous attempts of death, accidents, sickness and the most powerful witchdoctors. When we had to pass through deep waters, we were not drowned, nor were we burnt when we were going through the fire.

I was raised in a Christian home but I never had a true relationship with Jesus. My dad was a staunched Catholic and back then we had to attend the Roman Catholic Church. I had to attend Catechism and say the Rosary. I could say the Hail Mary even in my sleep. Every Sunday morning the family would leave early to attend 'Mass' which became rather boring for me except when we had visitors, or my class boys helped to serve Holy Communion. It was fun to watch the mistakes they made while they helped Father Dominic. Mass had become boring. I was tired of taking communion with no reverence to Jesus dying on the cross for our sins and confessing my sins to a priest. Deep within me, I knew there was more than going to church every Sunday and returning home quite the same. I earnestly believed that I would find satisfaction for my soul and yearning heart outside of the Catholic Church. I had the longing to

THE PURPOSE BEHIND THE PROBLEM

have a closer relationship with Jesus and had even refused to make my Confirmation by making an excuse that I did not have a suitable dress. Two days later, when I returned from school, I found a white dress with a pair of white shoes on my bed. I grew up in a home where my dad made decisions and we had to submit to whatever he said. Although our home was devoted to the Roman Catholic Church, I continually longed for reality, even from my youth. Many of my friends were already experiencing the joys of being teenagers, while I was cooped up at home, learning to cook and clean house so I rebelled against my parents like any teenager would. I became friends with the wrong crowd, who influenced me to drink, party, and go to clubs and disobey the rules of my parents. When I discovered how much my rebellion and disobedience was hurting my mom, I vowed to myself that I would never be like my friends. God knew my heart and the longing I had to know Him and when I was invited to a Gospel crusade, He changed my life.

It was during the ministering of the Word that God began to convict me of my sins. I sat there and felt like I was on the operating table. God had cut me open so I could see what my life was like without Him. He wanted to make me a new creation. My heart began to beat so fast. I knew that the Lord was speaking to me, that He was knocking at my hearts door and I had to take the decision to let Him in. I looked around in the tent, saw many of my high school friends, and knew they mocked whoever went up for prayer after the altar call. After the preacher shared the Word, he made an altar call. I began

THE PURPOSE BEHIND THE PROBLEM

to feel very uncomfortable and my heart kept beating faster and faster. It was as if the preacher was patiently waiting for me because he kept looking in my direction and repeating, "There is still some young people that need to come to the front, God is calling you to surrender your life to Him." My heartbeat was so fast by now that I could hardly breathe. The preacher repeated, "God is calling you He is speaking to you right now." My heart began to beat faster and faster. I clung to my chair but it did not help. I felt like something was pushing me out of my chair and the more I resisted, the more uncomfortable I became. The next thing I found myself on the stage and gave my heart to Jesus.

Giving my heart to the Lord was the best thing ever, I felt so pure, so spotlessly clean, so holy. I will never forget the blessing and the glory of being cleansed and justified by the blood of Jesus. This was the most wonderful experience I had ever had in my life. A deep settled holy peace came into my soul, the everlasting peace of God. I had found the very pure, holy joy of God that filled my innermost being. I was a new creation. 2 Corinthians 5:17 *anyone who is joint to Christ is a new being.*

I started going to a church called Antioch Assembly and systematically I started learning what God required of me as a believer. I had such a hunger to learn more about Jesus. I would sit with the Bible and read not being able to understand and one day, out of frustration I asked the Lord to help me understand His Word. The next day I was so surprised that I could understand what I was reading. This is how I started my walk as a believer in

THE PURPOSE BEHIND THE PROBLEM

Christ. The Holy Spirit was my teacher. I did Bible Studies on my own with the help of the Holy Spirit and never went to Bible School. I even burnt my book of pop songs and started listening to gospel music. God saved my family as well. My eldest brother, John, would come over with his guitar and the family would gather around and sing. Oh, those are happy memories.
When I was about sixteen years old, I had a beautiful dream of children of all ages and culture surrounding me. My pastor had interpreted my dream as a vision to my calling, to work with children. A few months later, I was teaching Sunday school and no matter where I found myself, I enjoyed myself best when I was among little children. Looking back to the year I gave my heart to the Lord, I realized that God had a plan and a purpose for my life. Ephesians 2:10 explains it so clearly *that before the world began, God chose me in Christ Jesus for specific kingdom works, now that I am born again, the Holy Spirit will empower me to fulfill them.*

The most important thing I have learnt is that, being a Christian in Christ means being continuously on an exciting, joyful and often daunting journey sometimes filled with sorrow and pain. It is an ongoing learning and growing process. As I grew in the Lord my understanding of who God is and the role He plays in our lives became clearer. Previously I used to blame God for everything that went wrong in my life.

I must have been about 14 years old when my younger sister passed away. I could not believe that a loving and caring God could let someone die. I was devastated. I

THE PURPOSE BEHIND THE PROBLEM

hated my sister for dying and leaving me to face the pain. I could not stand to see my mother grieving and in pain. I nursed and nurtured my hurt, blocked God out and mourned for days without allowing God to heal me. I later realized only God was able to heal me and send the comforter, the Holy Spirit to comfort me. God was able to fill the emptiness I had felt with His *agape* love and restore my joy.

The more I grew in the Lord, the more I realized that God never uses problems to punish us but He has a purpose behind every problem. He uses circumstances to develop our character. He sets the day of our birth and the day of our death and ordains everything that comes to pass in-between. God even uses incidents that may seem to us as senseless tragedies. Whether it is our best friend turning against us, being expelled from school or varsity, failing an exam after studying for hours, finding out about a fatal disease or sickness, going through a divorce or losing a job or a loved one, we should never blame God. God's ultimate purpose is to shape His children into the image of Jesus often using difficult moments and human tragedies. The book of Jonah in the Bible tells us that the Lord told Jonah to do something that he really did not feel like doing. Then Jonah tried to escape from the Lord but the Lord's call followed him everywhere. He ended up on a ship and was thrown overboard into the sea. He ended up in the belly of a huge fish. Only then he came to his senses and was prepared to do what the Lord called him to do.
So, if today you know that the Lord has called you to do something and you keep trying to run away from it, stop.

THE PURPOSE BEHIND THE PROBLEM

Stop running away and start running in God's direction. If the Lord has put you in a specific situation, stop trying to escape the pressures and start embracing them with all that is within you. As you do, the Lord will send you like He sent Jonah to where he needed to go. The Lord sent me to the Eastern Cape where I needed to be. God will form this character trait in you, just like He did it in my life. Trust the Lord that He knows very well what He is doing! As I look back upon my life, I realize I was the 'different' one in the family, always too scared to get into trouble, always tried to do what is right but still has landed up in trouble. I stood out from the rest of my brothers and sisters. I am the only one from the family today that is living out my calling. When I think of the countless times I almost died, was involved in fights and accidents and bewitched then I realize it is only through grace and mercy that I am still alive today. God had a reason for keeping me alive.

Joseph in the Bible, in the book of Genesis, saw the invisible Hand of God in his life. He understood that behind his conniving brothers, stood the Lord God who orchestrated the entire situation, to get him to the right place, at just the right moment to save his whole family. Though it took years and years for God's purpose to become clear, in the end Joseph saw the Hand of God behind everything that had happened to him. Look at the pattern.
At just the right moment, Joseph's brothers threw him into the pit. At just the right moment, the Ishmaelite's came along, at just the right moment, Joseph was sold to Potiphar, at just the right moment, and he was falsely

THE PURPOSE BEHIND THE PROBLEM

accused and thrown into jail. At just the right moment, he met the baker and the cupbearer, at just the right moment, Pharaoh called for Joseph. At just the right moment, Joseph was promoted to prime minister. At just the right moment, Jacob sent his sons to Egypt, at just the right moment, Pharaoh offered Joseph's family the land of Goshen and at just the right moment, they settled there and prospered. All these events happened at just the right moment and 'in just the right way' so the right people would be in the right place, at the right time. So that in the end, everything would be as God ordained it at the beginning.

Nothing happens anywhere in the universe by accident. God is at work in all things, at all times, to accomplish His will. When we come to believe that God is at work in our lives, at all times, we find rest in the confidence that He will work out our circumstances for the best. Remember it is not what happens to us, it is how we respond that makes the difference!

THE PURPOSE BEHIND THE PROBLEM

CHAPTER 6

Repaid for what the Locusts had Eaten

The ocean stretched out vast and beautiful before us, glittering in the morning sun. We had travelled the whole night but I was more excited than tired. We had finally reached Jeffrey's Bay, our place of destination according to God's plan. Candice was delighted to see us. She had phoned throughout the journey asking how far we were and now it all seemed like a dream when she finally came and picked us up.

I met the rest of my cousins. We spent enjoyable days on the beach as it was the festive season. Curious to see our new town, we took long walks along the beach into town and explored every shop. My favorite place was the Shell Museum. I loved the little crafts and ornaments made from shells, a result of long hours and hard work from the people who had made them. My first thought after Christmas was to get a job so my cousin's wife organized me a job at Checkers. I enjoyed working again, my dedication and hard work soon paid off, and I was promoted from cashier to the cash office as an office clerk. My duties included cashing up and doing the banking, handing out change to the cashiers, handling the payouts, petty cash and other general office duties. I worked most weekends and on public holidays and went to church, when I was off work. One day as I was busy doing the banking; I discovered that exactly R1000.00

THE PURPOSE BEHIND THE PROBLEM

was missing. I freaked out. I counted and re-counted the money. I checked the entire cashier cashing up slips against those on the computer, checked the safe, checked the petty cash- nothing! I called my supervisor and we re-counted and checked everything but could not find the mistake. I went home almost in tears.
That night I turned to God in prayer "Lord Jesus please show me where the mistake is. Father, you know that I am innocent and if the money is not found, I will be in trouble so please Lord, answer my cry."

God did answer me but not the way in which I had hoped. God reminded me of the day I had been uncomfortable at work, when I was fed up and had the sudden feeling just to leave work. I had ignored the feeling, thinking it was because I had moved house and was not familiar with the area but it was not that. After a few days, I just continued hoping that the feeling would pass and things would return to normal not realizing that, that was God speaking to me. I had tried to shrug off the feeling and in turn wrestled against God and disobeyed Him. Suddenly it dawned on me- God had allowed it to happen to get my attention. What was God trying to say to me? I was already scheduled to attend a hearing the next day. I was even prepared to take the lie detector test because I knew I was innocent. That night I could not sleep, I went on my knees and asked God what it was that He wanted me to do. Then it became as clear as day. God had closed the door to my previous job so I could work for Him…what was I doing working at Checkers? I cried and repented. I told God I was ready to be obedient, to be led by Him and do what He wanted me to

THE PURPOSE BEHIND THE PROBLEM

do. I had to accept that I was no longer going to be working at Checkers.

I attended the hearing and was offered my job back, I was found innocent. A payout slip was found behind the petty cash box to the value of R999.99 but I decided to do what the Lord instructed me. I knew what I had to do this time. I said good-bye to management and the staff as I proudly walked out the door with a smile on my face. I knew my husband was not going to understand but I knew he was going to come around once he realized I was on God's mandate.

When we realize life is a test, nothing is insignificant in our lives. Even the smallest incident can develop our character. I surrendered my life totally into God's hands. I attended every church service at the Assemblies of God church and God began to take me through spiritual experiences that brought blessings over my life. I remember the day the Lord paid us a visit but it was not in glory and splendor. Our property owner had put us out simply because she wanted to open a tuck-shop and use the building we were renting. We had to be out by the afternoon. We had nowhere to go. I was heartbroken. We were new to Jeffrey's Bay and hardly knew anybody. Where would we start looking? Enver felt so helpless when our belongings eventually ended up on the street. My children cried and said we must go back home to Kwazulu- Natal. Through my tears in prayer, I asked God why, repeatedly. I had the feeling to walk down the road and met someone who I knew from another church. She saw that I was troubled and after explaining to her, she took me to her sister's house four blocks away. It

THE PURPOSE BEHIND THE PROBLEM

seemed that God was already in control as Mrs. Natal offered me the keys to her place that was fully furnished and vacant, without asking us for a cent. We moved in and had a roof over our heads that night. God never let us down. The next morning, I found Rene Natal, our new property owner, at the door. I assumed she was coming to talk money for the rent, but once again, God blew me totally away by what He did. The property owner gave me all the furniture and everything that was in her house. A lounge suite, dining room set, coffee table, a big double door fridge, dishes and pots, crockery and cutlery, a double bed with a dressing table and bedding and curtains. I could not hold back the tears; this time it was tears of joy. I could not stop thanking God, touched deeply by what He had done. God had used a bad situation to bring forth a blessing and display His greatness and glory. My mind recalled the study on closed doors and open doors. God definitely closed one door to open an improved one. God also brought to my memory the prophetic word (Joel 2:25) He had promised that he would *repay me for the years the locusts had eaten*. God had replaced all our things we had to sell when He spoke to me about moving to Jeffrey's Bay.

As long as God is on the throne, there is no situation that is beyond His control. His love has no limit and His provision has no measure. For out of his infinite riches in Jesus, He is able to give again and again.

THE PURPOSE BEHIND THE PROBLEM

CHAPTER 7

Heaven or Hell

I woke up terrified and crying. I could still see them screaming, tormented as the worms came out of their bodies from every opening. Their screams were filled with anguish, pain and torment as they tried in vain to escape the flames. Tattoos of eagles, snakes, rats, chains and other images that were on the bodies of some of these people became alive and started tormenting them. I gasped in shock as I saw a large bird that a man had tattooed on his back, now pecking at his flesh, half of his nose had already been pecked away as he cried in pain and anger. The scripture in the Bible in *Leviticus 19:28* came to my mind, *"Ye shall not make any cuttings in your flesh for the dead, nor print or tattoo any marks upon you: I am the Lord."* I saw young and old, people of every race, culture and denomination tormented and screaming and I wept and trembled as I realized that no one could help them, not even God. They had rejected Him and now it was too late, they were paying for their sinful deeds on earth. I saw people reaching their arms out for help but alas, the flames would drown them and their flesh would burn and fall off piece by piece as the worms would appear and fill their bodies. They would scream and cry in vain with no one to rescue them from the lake of fire.

THE PURPOSE BEHIND THE PROBLEM

Something happened to me after God had given me just this tiny glimpse of hell. Besides me being terrified and in tears, I realized just how real hell is. Yes, we all believe there is heaven and there is a hell but when we face the reality of what hell is really all about, we would be so moved to tell the lost about Jesus and the price He paid for our salvation, saving them from the place of darkness where there will be weeping and gnashing of teeth as God Word tells us in *Matthew 25:28*.

We, as human beings cannot save, deliver or redeem anybody but God can use us as His 'vessels' or 'instruments' to tell the world about Jesus and though the convicting power of God's Holy Spirit, they can come to repentance and receive salvation through accepting Jesus into their lives. *Luke 16:19-31* records the words of Jesus as He spoke about certain rich man who came into daily contact with a poor man called Lazarus. The rich man lived a life of luxury whilst Lazarus was so poor that he would not even have minded eating the breadcrumbs from the rich man's table. Jesus says the rich man went to hell. He may have been a well-respected man in the community because of his riches but because he ignored the desperate needs of the poor man that was starving and dying on his doorstep, he went to hell where he was in torment. He calls to Lazarus to dip his finger in water and cool his tongue because he was in agony in the fire.

Hell is a place of torment:
(1) Hell was designed originally for Satan and his demons (Matthew 25:41; Revelation 20:10).

THE PURPOSE BEHIND THE PROBLEM

(2) Hell will also punish the sin of those who reject Christ (Matthew 13:41, 50; Revelation 20:11-15; 21:8).
(3) Hell is conscious torment.
- Matthew 13:50 *"furnace of fire...weeping and gnashing of teeth"*
- Mark 9:48 *"where their worm does not die, and the fire is not quenched"*
- Revelation 14:10 *"he will be tormented with fire and brimstone"*

(4) Hell is eternal and irreversible.
- Revelation 14:11 *"the smoke of their torment goes up forever and ever and they have no rest day and night"*
- Revelation 20:14 *"This is the second death, the lake of fire"*
- Revelation 20:15 *"If anyone's name was not found written in the book of life, he was thrown into hell*

Hell is real and existing. We may have heard of hell and think it is just a matter of getting there, burning, screaming a little bit and dying, end of story but it is not. The scriptures above clearly show that hell is eternal. Matthew 13:40 warns us *the Son of Man (Jesus) will send out his angels and they will collect all the sinners and throw them into a fiery furnace (hell) where there will be weeping and gnashing of teeth.* Friend, if you have rejected Jesus, then there is no way you can escape hell. God's word says *all those whose names are not written in the Book of Life will be thrown into the Lake of Fire.*
Is your name written in the Book of Life?

THE PURPOSE BEHIND THE PROBLEM

1John 3:8 *He that committeth sin is of the devil. There is no other way to obtain salvation but in and through Jesus* Acts 4:12.
No doctor, no medicine, no man, no preacher or priest, no church can save you from sin, only Jesus the Lamb of God that taketh away the sins of the world, can save you by His blood and by the power of His Spirit. So many people go to church, read and believe God's Word, profess to know Jesus but I want to tell you that if you have not accepted Jesus as your personal Saviour, if you have not asked Jesus to take your sinful heart and cleanse it with His precious blood and forgive you for your sins, and committed your life to serving and loving Him, then you are headed for hell.
Isaiah 42:6-7 Jesus said *whosoever committeth sin is the servant of sin but if the Son of God shall make you free, you are free indeed.*

Barabbas was a sinner and a murderer who was condemned to death. He was to be crucified, but Jesus took his place and carried the cross on which Barabbas should have died. Jesus the Son of God was crucified in the place of Barabbas, in your place and in my place; the murderer was set free because another one had died his death. You and I am that Barabbas. *The wages of sin is death but the gift of God is eternal life through Jesus Christ.* If you look in faith to the cross of Christ, you will see yourself and your sin nailed to the cross. Jesus has taken your place on the cross that you may live forever. *For God so loved the world that he gave his only begotten Son (Jesus) that you may not die (spiritually*

THE PURPOSE BEHIND THE PROBLEM

and end up in hell) but have everlasting life (in heaven with Jesus.

You can invite Jesus into your life right now, you do not have to be in a church or with a minister or in a fancy holy place. Just ask God to forgive you by telling him all your sins (it is called repentance) and ask him to cleanse your heart with His precious blood. Then invite Him into your heart and He will do the rest.
Trevor Goddard, the well-known and popular ex-captain of the South African cricket team once said *when it comes to having Jesus in your life, He does not want to be the resident, and He wants to be the PRESIDENT.* In other words, it's not good enough to just have Jesus in your life 'Jesus needs to be the very essence of your being, your absolute priority, the One who is ruling and reigning in your life.'
When it comes to following Jesus, it really is a case of *all or nothing.* He wants to have absolute pre-eminence in our lives. He desires to be not only your Savior but also your Lord.
The choice is yours. Do you choose heaven or hell?

THE PURPOSE BEHIND THE PROBLEM

CHAPTER 8
Transformed by Trouble

For months I was out of a job. Leaving work at Checkers made it possible for me to join the sisters at A.O.G. (Assemblies of God) church who were on a sacrificial fast. We fasted for 30 days and abstained from the things we loved. For those 30 days, we ate no meat at all, drank no tea or coffee, and never watched any TV shows. At the end of the fast, we had to give someone our favorite set of clothing. It was hard for me to let go of my favorite brown leather boots. We were instructed to read the book of Matthew in the Bible. When I had completed all 28 chapters, the Lord led me to read the book of Job. As I studied Job's lifestyle and struggles and identified with his situation, I could feel that something spiritually supernatural was happening within me. God took me to a higher spiritual dimension.

There were times when my cupboards were empty, when I had no bread for my hungry children, when my husband and I were both out of work, when he drank and he stressed me out, when my children became disobedient and stubborn that God reminded me of what Job went through. He went through so much hurt and pain, sickness, struggles and problems, lost all his children and livestock but he never forsook the Lord. He never gave up even when his wife, of all people, told him to curse God and rather die. How many of us choose to stay at the feet of Jesus when we face struggles and problems? How many of us turn against God? Job bore

THE PURPOSE BEHIND THE PROBLEM

his suffering until God blessed him and gave him back double all he had lost. Yes, maybe there were days when he complained and cried out to God. I quote *"I can't be quiet, I am angry and bitter, and I have to speak."* (Job 7:11) He cried out when God seemed distant. Job's lifestyle has taught me that God can handle our doubt, our anger, grief, confusion and questions. Sometimes admitting our hopelessness can turn into a step of faith. Sometimes we wonder how can we praise God when we do not understand what is happening in our lives. The answer is simply to trust God even though nothing makes sense. Job held onto God's Word and this helped him to remain faithful. His faith was so strong in the midst of pain that he was able to pass the test.

Job's situation and his trust in God rubbed off on me. I began to remember what God had already done for me and refused to be moved by my financial situation. Even when I received the news that I had to move out of the house, I began to trust God in spite of my situation and my feelings and worshipped him in the deepest way. I refused to be troubled by trouble. I knew I could trust God to keep His promise during my time of famine and dryness. I knew I had to patiently rely on the promises of God and realize He is taking me to a deeper level of maturity to live out my calling. I realized that men and women who were made aware of their calling from the Lord discovered that carrying out that call and arriving at that place of service was downright painful and full of surprises. Look at Abraham, he was asked to sacrifice his son, Isaac. His mission was plainly stated and clearly communicated by the Lord, but in the final analysis, God

THE PURPOSE BEHIND THE PROBLEM

was testing him all the time having other plans in mind. So how can I complain when God knows what he is doing with me? David, in the Bible was anointed to become king of Israel but he became the object of King Saul's jealousy and wrath. For years the pressure he endured mounted to such an extent that I am sure he wondered if he was to see the day he would become king. Poor Hosea, his life was a real scandal, yet he was under the Lord's direction when he married the adulterous Gomer, taking her back after her continued unfaithfulness. Joseph's life inspires me. He was maligned mistreated and falsely accused yet this was God's chosen will for him as His vessel.
God is not looking us over for medals, degrees and diplomas but for scars.

That very day I let God have his way with my life for nothing is worse than resisting and resenting the One who is at work with you and in you. The Holy Spirit helped me to go deeper into God's word, into prayer, not just praying prayers of petition or asking God to meet my need but spending intimate, dynamic time with Him to receive guidance and direction for my life. God then brought to pass many of the prophecies that were spoken over my life. This gave me hope and I refused to be moved by circumstances and situations. I told the devil I refuse to give up or to quit, I will stick around and face my mountain and keep on striving until I found a mountain pass or maybe a tunnel but I refused to quit. God had brought me too far for me to turn back and with God's help; I was ready to turn my mountain into a gold mine.

THE PURPOSE BEHIND THE PROBLEM

God strengthened me as I fasted daily. He was faithful and met my needs. Not once did my family go to bed without food. When I attended service one evening, this was the word for me. Habakkuk 2 v 17-19 *though the fig tree does not bud, and there are no grapes on the vines, though the olive crop fails and the fields produce no food, though there are no sheep in the pen and no cattle in the stalls, yet I will rejoice in the Lord. I will be joyful in God my Savior.* I felt God was saying to me. "Wait- and while you wait rejoice! I am Your Provider and I will bless you though everything looks bare and fruitless around you, just trust me." When last did you receive a word from the Lord? God was teaching me a valuable lesson- to wait! Learning to wait is a test of maturity. Waiting does force us to recognize we are not in control, God is. It humbles us in ways, which we need to be humbled. Moses waited 80 years for a ministry that only lasted 40 years- two thirds of his life was spent waiting and getting ready. I realized that God said that the plans He had for me are good so I decided to trust God and wait.

God gave me a passion for souls. I started evangelizing with a sister from the church. We would go house to house telling people about God's great love, Jesus purpose for dying on the cross for humanity and we would pray for their healing and their needs. We shared our testimonies with young and old making sure that they do not listen to our one-sided stories of success with no mention of failure and become discouraged. Sometimes people think that while they struggle, we

THE PURPOSE BEHIND THE PROBLEM

have it all. We must be careful not to falsify the records and fail to tell the truth. There is no one that is righteous. We *were* saved by grace, we *are* saved by grace and we *will* always be saved by grace. It was after Paul filled jails and graves with believers that he wrote, "I owe a great debt." (Romans 1:14) then went on to impact the whole world with the Gospel.

With God, there is no limit. When we hand over everything that distracts us from our Savior, not only is our spiritual experience deepened and enriched, but our entire life becomes filled with the awareness of His presence. There is no richer experience in life than this.

THE PURPOSE BEHIND THE PROBLEM

CHAPTER 9

Surrender and Obedience

I realized that God is far more concerned with our journey than he is with our destination. He wants us to have an intimate and holy relationship with Him so He can teach us and show us things. Even if it takes a little longer than anticipated, then that is perfectly fine with Him. He loves to marinade because he wants our hearts to be tender and willing. Two most important things I had learnt on my life journey were: to *surrender* and *wait*. God is able to work wonders with a surrendered heart and waiting upon the Lord, renews our strength.

I was waiting upon the Lord to open a door for me, as I was still not working. One Sunday as I placed a R10.00 into the offering basket, I trusted in God for financial breakthrough. The next day a sister in the Lord called me from Port Elizabeth. She had deposited R100.00 into my bank account. I went to the ATM to draw the money and what I discovered made me break down in tears. When you have no money at all and someone gives you even a lousy little R10.00 it means so much. I was surprised to find there was R539.00 in my account! I stood in front of that ATM and said a silent prayer of thanks to the Lord. I knew that I had not a cent in my account and that this was truly a miracle from God. If God knows the number of hairs we have on our heads, then surely He knows our phone numbers and bank account numbers as well.

THE PURPOSE BEHIND THE PROBLEM

My waiting period was over and I started teaching Sunday school at A.O.G church. A week later, I received a call from Victory4All Christian School asking me to come in for an interview. After the interview, I was taken and shown around the school. I was shown to my classroom and even met some of the kids who would be in my class. I was so excited. Two days later, I received a message that I was no longer needed, that they had taken someone else. Closed door! I was heart-sore and very disappointed. Once again, the study on closed and open doors came to mind and I realized God had a better door in store for me. One thing I had learnt was never to fight a closed door. Once again, I surrendered to the Lord and remembered the portion of scripture in Acts about Paul and Timothy who saw the need to go and preach the Gospel in Asia. They were however forbidden to do so by the Holy Spirit (Acts 16:6-8) then they tried to go to Bithynia but again they were not permitted to do so. These two eager Christians felt that it will be good for the people in Asia and Bithynia to hear the good news about Jesus but it was not the *purpose* of God for Paul and Timothy *at that time.* Had they been insensitive and pushed through this 'closed door' who knows what the consequences may have been. It is important to remember that God will only anoint us for ministry that he has directed us to do. How many times have we believed God for healing and after He had healed us, we still took medication not realizing that God had already closed the door to that illness in our lives but we forced it open again. We need to surrender to God.

THE PURPOSE BEHIND THE PROBLEM

Surrender is best demonstrated by obedience and trust. Jesus surrendered to God's plans the night before His crucifixion. Genuine surrender says "Father, if this problem, pain, brokenness or circumstance is needed to fulfill Your purpose and glory in my life or in another's, please do not take it away."

After I surrendered, I experienced peace. When Joshua encountered the biggest battle of his life, he encountered God and fell in worship before him and surrendered his plans. That surrender caused the stunning victory at Jericho. Surrendered people are the ones God uses. We *must* surrender to God.
Luke 5:4-5 warns us to hearken unto God's Word. *'Master we have worked hard all night and haven't caught anything" Peter said "But because you say so, I will let down the nets."* Peter was an excellent fisherman; he had been at his profession for a very long time. After all, he made his living that way. After a long night of fishing and catching nothing, he was ready to hang up the nets and go home for a good sleep.
However, Jesus had other plans "Put out into the deep water and put down the nets for a catch" He told Peter. Peter could have argued "I am the fisherman around here. You do the preaching and I will do the fishing okay" but he surrendered his pride and his tiredness to Jesus.
"Because you say so, I will let down the nets" he said. The result! They caught such a large amount of fish that their nets began to break. Sometimes what God wants us to do does not make sense. It does not seem to be the right timing or the right thing to do. Still, if God is

speaking to us, we do not need to understand, surrender and obedience is what counts.

All too often, our prayers in times of difficulty boil down to three words 'Change my situation.' While praying like this is not wrong, it can sometimes lead us in a wrong direction. If we take Psalm 119 in the Bible seriously, we ought to pray "Lord, teach me your word." If we know the Word, then we can pray the Word into our situation and allow God to take control. Instead, we sometimes say "Lord, change my marriage or get me out of it, change my boss, change my husband, change my wife." Often we want things to change. God's Word to us is sometimes to *wait, endure, be patient and persevere* which is why long-suffering is a fruit of the Spirit.

God was teaching me vital life lessons here. God taught me to persevere. Suffering produces perseverance and perseverance produces character that in turn produces hope and hope does not disappoint us. (Romans 3:4) God called me to rejoice in my pain. *Consider it pure joy my brothers and sisters whenever you face many kinds of trials because you know that the testing of your faith, develops perseverance. Perseverance must finish your work so that you may be mature and complete, not lacking anything.* James 1:2-4

God reminded me of the Potter and the clay. The clay does not question the Potter because the Potter knows what shape He wants the clay to be, and if the clay does not look right, the Potter will remold and reshape the clay until He is satisfied with what He has made. How can the clay resist the Potter and try to slip out of His

THE PURPOSE BEHIND THE PROBLEM

hands- this will make the molding process take much longer and make it more and more difficult. Nevertheless, when the clay submits to the Potter, the process is quick and less painful.

I learnt many things about God during this time. I learnt that He knew what I was going through. He used my trials to help me grow and that He is faithful even in my troubles. He is involved in everything that happened to me.

THE PURPOSE BEHIND THE PROBLEM

CHAPTER 10

I have Plans for you Arise!

The Lord is good! Sometimes the Lord's goodness is seen quickly, other times it is seen slowly. Eventually we realize that nothing leaves the Lord's hand that does not touch His goodness in one way or another. I knew that God was preparing me for something great as I faced a challenge each new day. I was house hunting, as I had to move out from the house we were living in. I knew the best thing to do was to pray and surrender this problem to God. God promised in Psalm 50:15 *Call to me when trouble comes; I will save you, and you will praise me.* I knew for a fact that there were no vacant houses. God specializes in impossible situations, so I left my situation in His mighty hands. In addition, if I thought I had my hands full with that, Cameron, my son, disappeared and did not come home. When he did not return the day thereafter, I began to get worried and thought something had happened to him. I must have asked a thousand 'why' questions that day and hardly slept that night. I prayed almost the whole night.

The next day Enver showed me our local newspaper with a picture of the street children. Guess who was with them? My son, Cammy. I was hurt, angry and shocked. I immediately took the paper and went to the police station and the police agreed to bring him home because they

THE PURPOSE BEHIND THE PROBLEM

knew all the hideouts of the street children. I went home, waited until the evening and finally went to bed, deciding to go back to the station the next day.

I prayed- the tears just rolling, how could he? How can he disappear from home? What was he doing on the street? What made him do it? Why is it that the people who pray, who teach their kids right from wrong, who fear God and live righteously, are the one's going through the most hurt and pain? It was because Satan knew the only way he could get to me was by using my son. I just asked God to do His job and continued to pray.

A little later, Enver told me the police were outside. God never let me down. They had found Cammy and had brought him home. I was so grateful that he was okay and alive. He refused to talk or to answer any of my questions so I just prayed over him and that night I had a good sleep after many sleepless nights. A few days later, he disappeared again. My heart broke. I notified the police and they assured me they will bring him home.

A sister from our church needed some help at J/Bay Laundry where she worked and I agreed to help her out for a week. With the money, I was able to buy the props and costumes I needed for the Sunday school Christmas play. One afternoon on my way from work, I passed some broken down buildings in St Croix Street and saw some children playing outside. They were untidy and dirty. I called them to speak to them but they ran into the broken building to hide. I went home troubled and wondered where Cammy was and what he was doing.

THE PURPOSE BEHIND THE PROBLEM

Every day as I passed these buildings, the urge to speak to these kids became stronger and stronger and I wondered if I would ever get the opportunity to tell them about Jesus' love and to find out where Cammy was.

That weekend our church had a whole night prayer and all I prayed about was for Cammy to come back home. He was only 15 years old. Apart from his brother, he was the quiet, obedient child who never complained when he was asked to do a task. Did I perhaps not love him enough or show him that I loved him just as much as Tyrell? Was it something that I had said to him? God knew the pain I was experiencing to see my child whom I had dedicated to Him, who grew up in church, snatched away by the devil and his evil forces. God spoke to me through 1 Peter 4:16-19 *to count my sufferings for Christ a joy, no matter what I go through.*

Many nights when I went to bed devastated, not knowing where Cammy was or with who- and most of the times I was angry at myself because I felt there was nothing I could do to help him because I did not know where he was. My heart bled for weeks because I could not understand why this was happening. I prayed for Cammy every single night. Even the police could not find him. Many times I would examine my life and even ask God what I have done wrong to deserve this. Every time when I wanted answers and when I was confused, when I felt the load I was carrying was, becoming too much to bear- that still voice inside would assure me that there is hope- that as long as the door is still ajar, it is not closed. It will stay open.

THE PURPOSE BEHIND THE PROBLEM

During this time of 'suffering' I began to pray the most authentic, most heartfelt-honest-to-God prayers. God assured me through His Word once again, that there was a plan, a purpose and a reason for Cammy's disappearance. God could have kept Joseph out of jail, He could have kept Daniel out of the lion's den, kept Paul from shipwreck, kept the three Hebrew boys from being thrown into the fiery furnace- but He did not. He let those problems happen and every one of these people was drawn closer to God as a result. Even Jeremiah was thrown into a slimy pit for a reason. Problems force us to look to God and depend on Him instead of ourselves. God allows certain things to happen to us that He will use either to prune, shape and mold us or to bring glory to His name. God made me realize that He never changes the plans He has for us. He will stick to His original plan to get us to where He wants us no matter what Satan may try to do.

The Lord made me realize that Cammy was not alone, he was somewhere with all the other street children. Suddenly I realized that there must be a reason for these kids to be living on the streets. Why would they run away from home? Where do they sleep and what do they eat?
I suddenly found myself consigned to this assignment of finding out more about the street children and the reasons why they were living on the streets and not at home. I prayed and asked the Lord to connect me with the right parents. I needed to hear the truth and not some sugar-coated version of how tough life is that parents cannot send their children to school.

THE PURPOSE BEHIND THE PROBLEM

Some of the people were very helpful and spoke the truth. Drugs were the main problem and most of the parents were addicts as well. No wonder the kids were running away from home. It worried me that children so young, who were supposed to be at, school, were wandering on the streets.
I realized that so many innocent little children were being deprived of love, neglected and abused. They were deprived of respect and education by parents who have either abandoned them, or fallen prey to Satan's trap of bondage of alcoholism and drugs. Parents who take their children's social grant money to buy alcohol and not food- these little children were suffering. For the first time, I felt something arising in me that wanted me to protect these children. Then there were the street children who were involved in drugs and crime. My heart went out for them- some have never been to school, they cannot read or write. They have never received love from their parents so they look for it elsewhere and end up on the streets, doing wrong. Every time I prayed about this, something happened to me that I could not explain. I felt their loneliness and rejection and pain – they were trying to fill the emptiness in their lives with crime and depended on getting high to escape reality.

I now realized why God had allowed Cammy to be part of them; to get my attention and for me to become involved. I had already spoken to some parents about having Prayer meetings to pray for these children. I knew that people sometimes did not worry about others- as long as they had food, a roof over their heads and

THE PURPOSE BEHIND THE PROBLEM

money then everything was all right. Another issue that bothered me was children that were being abused by their male relatives, their uncles, fathers and stepfathers? I am talking about sexual abuse- it was going to affect them for the rest of their lives.
Whenever I prayed, I asked for God's protection upon all the vulnerable children who were faced with this situation.
I had developed such a passion to work with and help these children. It was as if the Lord had suddenly opened my eyes to see and realize the issues these kids were facing. If only I had a place, where I could put them all under one roof and tell them Jesus loves them.

God made me understand that many of these children had been spiritually 'broken.' They chose to live on the streets because they did not fit in with other children. Some of them were emotionally 'dead' because of the mental and physical abuse they had endured. They did not care about taking care of themselves or about the clothes; they wore because they felt dirty, unworthy and unclean on the inside. Some of them felt inhuman and thought it was okay for them to be abused because this was happening at home. Some of them had been hurt, abused, maybe even raped, molested, traumatized and their spirits have been damaged and they need healing. A familiar proverb says 'as the tree is bent, so the tree grows.' If a child of two years falls and breaks a leg which does not mend because the bone is not set properly, the child may limp for the rest of her life. People sometimes limp emotionally throughout their lives from incidents like abuse, molestation, rape,

THE PURPOSE BEHIND THE PROBLEM

abduction, hurt, hate and pain from which they are not set free. Also, from sinful moments and other emotional issues. Jesus sternly rebuked the Pharisees to first clean the inside of the dish/cup. If our spirits are damaged, how can we love God and receive love from Him to give to ourselves and others?

Some pointers from my studies.[4] Came to mind and I remembered that the abuse of street drugs and repeated drunkenness are doorways for Satan to enter. Several youngsters have reported that they enter into a completely different world on their high (Satan's world) and sometimes they are completely controlled by Satan and his demons.

Child abuse usually results in demonic infestation. Abused children unless delivered, usually turn out to be child-abusing parents themselves.

Sexual intercourse is another big doorway because demons are passed from one person to another through sexual intercourse. This is because two people involved become one flesh (*1 Cor.6:16-18*) Fornication means sexual intercourse between a man and a woman who are *not* married to each other. This is why God has given His people so many commands not to have sexual intercourse between anyone who is not man and wife. It is for our protection from this kind of demonic infestation. Rape and violent sexual assault particularly in children, is another doorway. The doorway of inheritance is often an overlooked one; the sins of the father being passed down to the sons.

THE PURPOSE BEHIND THE PROBLEM

I did some research on the ways that children are influenced by evil spirits and found that occult influences are rampant in toys for small children as well as some of the cartoons on TV. Small children are imaginative and Satan knows if he can direct their imagination to the spirit world, they will quickly learn to see and communicate with his demons. Some children even have an imaginary friend who they can talk to all day long. I am sure most of us are familiar with this. According to studies, Rock music is Satan's music, carefully planned and carried out by him. Almost all rock stars have agreed to serve Satan in return for money and fame. Rock stars whose souls and lives have been destroyed are teaching untold millions of young people to serve Satan and to worship him. Satanic groups place satanic curses on rock music recorded. They do many incantations, which place demons on every CD or DVD of rock music sold. In recordings, the Satanists themselves are recorded in the background (masked by the overall noise of the music) doing chants and incantations to summon up more demons when the CD is played to afflict the person playing the music and anyone who is listening. The purpose of this is mind control. All rock records, CDs and DVDs, tarot cards, Ouija boards, etcetera, produce legal ground for demons to bring a continuing evil power in the house. We must realize that if our loved ones are demonically bound and blinded, we can talk to them for years about their need for Jesus but they will not understand us. We must not give up but pray for God to remove the demon that is causing the barrier. We must understand the wonderful position of power our Lord Jesus has placed us in

THE PURPOSE BEHIND THE PROBLEM

(Hebrews 4:16) so we are able to destroy all negative forces and powers through prayer. My heart goes out to every child that has been through a dramatic ordeal but is too afraid to even speak about it. All I want to do is be of assistance to the many parents who have lost control to manage their children and help them by standing in prayer with them. Jesus did say in His word that *we should pray for one another and carry each other's burdens*

THE PURPOSE BEHIND THE PROBLEM

CHAPTER 11

I Know The Plans I Have For You

I received this wonderful, powerful vision from the Lord. I was at a place, which had two large dormitories. There was also a large hall. Church services, meetings and the teaching of God's Word happened there. Youth and children who had been hurt, abused, raped, abandoned and rejected by their families and others came to stay there- orphans and widows, young people and old- they all came.
Young people were trained and sent out to take the Gospel to others while these 'broken' people received prayer and teachings on healing and recovery. In my vision, I saw people who surrendered their lives to the Lord, who were healed and set free, now ministering and sharing their testimony with others. The Lord sent people to sponsor this ministry (THROM) Teach, Heal and Reach Out Ministries and all the children who were living on the premises were able to have enough food. The Outreach team visited hospitals, old-age homes, crèches, schools and homes, sharing the gospel with everyone. Children and adults who were ill were brought to THROM where they received prayer daily for healing. People who were set free would then dedicate themselves as volunteers doing God's work, passionate, zealous and radical about working for God. In my vision, I saw people that I knew very well, children and youth

THE PURPOSE BEHIND THE PROBLEM

who were hurt in relationships, which were broken and abandoned and abused.

This vision replayed in my mind for a couple of days and whenever the Lord showed me this vision I would weep. Whenever I was washing the dishes, cooking, cleaning, or praying, I would be reminded of this vision and I would weep in the Lord's presence.

Suddenly I knew it was time- time for me to do God's work. I knew it was time for God to take over my life. I gave the Lord permission for his Will to be done in my life and place me where He wants me to be. I was 100% sure it was time for me to stop applying for jobs and do what God brought me for to Jeffrey's Bay. It was time for me to step out of the boat and allow God to accomplish His will for my life.

After the Lord had shown me this vision I could no longer sit idle or let a day's pass by without fulfilling the urgency that had built up in my spirit to start working for God. I knew I was ready and was willing to serve wherever the Lord placed me. I was filled with the urge to go to the Joshua Project and my obedience led me to chat to Michelle Dorfling. I found myself sharing my testimony and the urge to work with kids who are broken and hurting. She told me she had prayed that very same morning for God to send in people and there I was. I knew this was no coincidence and felt like crying as I felt the warmth of God's holy love. This was indeed the work of God – He had led me to the right place at the right time. He knew where He had reserved a place for me and I thanked and praised Him all the way home as

THE PURPOSE BEHIND THE PROBLEM

He flooded my soul with joy. Two days later, I started work at the Joshua Project.

Connecting with the children came naturally. I felt in my heart that this was where I belonged. Nothing gave me more satisfaction than seeing a child's face light up after a tight hug or reaching out and helping those who needed help. The Lord grew me spiritually and I was able to pick up when children arrived troubled and needed spiritual help. One particular day, as I took a group of children to the classroom upstairs, a little girl began to cry. I immediately sensed that something was wrong. She seemed to be in pain while climbing the stairs. I took her downstairs and spoke to her privately, called her sister and discovered that a relative had sexually abused her. My heart broke. Instantly I felt anger arising within me. I wanted to strangle the person that did this to her but God reminded me that he loved the sinner but hated the sin. I arranged for a home visit and that little girl was referred for counseling.

The love I had for the kids was now accompanied by compassion and I was able to reach out to the kids that were hurting. I remembered from my studies, that when we repress our hurts, we are choosing to lie to ourselves. Oh, what tangible webs we weave when we practice to deceive. When we fail to admit to our consciousness, what our spirit faithfully sends up, we build a web of dishonesty. That is why children deprived of affection sometimes-later start to do mean things. This happens in the best homes repeatedly. Each time the child has to handle the hurt somehow; his spirit becomes more and more loaded. His emotions are no longer out in the open,

THE PURPOSE BEHIND THE PROBLEM

he has built a hiding place within himself. In the beginning, his walls are flexible but they become increasingly strong and rigid as the pressure of repressed emotions increase. The spirit and soul must have touch, light, laughter, joy, tears and excitement. Spirit and soul is not a machine or *thing* apart from the body. The child's spirit must have his own mother and father whenever possible- not substitutes.

Something even changed in my teaching Sunday school. Some of the bigger kids shared their troubles and hurts and I was able to come before the Lord and cry out to Him for their situation. I did not worry so much about Cammy anymore because I knew that while I was helping other children, that God was taking care of his problem. While I prayed for Cammy, every single day to return home, God was teaching me to let go. God met my daily needs and He granted Enver a job.

It was a Friday night and past eleven o' clock when Enver got out of bed and went and watched television. I was drifting off to sleep when suddenly I felt his hand on my shoulder. "Cameron is here and wants to talk to you" he told me. I got out of bed and Cammy came into the room sobbing "Mummy I'm sorry, I was in bed sleeping but something told me to come home and I was restless and could not sleep." By now, he was shaking as he sobbed and I put my arms around him and held him tight and told him that I forgive him. He signaled to the lounge, to Enver, and I told him to go and ask for forgiveness as well. Then I realized God had woken Enver up because I would never have heard Cammy

THE PURPOSE BEHIND THE PROBLEM

knocking. As they were talking and making peace, I realized that Cammy had arrived home on his own this time. The Holy Spirit must have been wrestling with him and God had seen my tears because I never let a day go by without crying out to the Lord for him. God had answered my prayer. I gave Cammy something to eat and went to bed just thanking God.

Cammy then got sick- his feet were swollen. Like any concerned mother, I took him to the clinic and all his tests were all negative. Whatever it was, I knew the only way to destroy it was through prayer. I prayed for him daily. It was heart sore to see him crying every morning because he could not even walk to the toilet without experiencing pain. Every day his feet would swell more and more. At first, I could not understand why the swelling would not go down, after I had prayed for several days. Only then, I began to understand that God was using this to teach Cammy a lesson and teach me a lesson as well. *Train up your child in the way he should go*.... We take this as a command to shape our children in the way *we* think they should go. That is not what it says. 'Train up your child in the way *he* should go' is a call to us to die to our own pictures of what we want our children to be, so that *through us,* the Father may call forth what He has created *them* to become. From that day, I released Cammy into God's hands and allowed God to have His way in his life.

God answered my prayer two weeks later after he told me to mix some salt and oil and anoint Cammy's feet. I then understood that the swelling had prevented him from running away from home again.

THE PURPOSE BEHIND THE PROBLEM

God started using me in the area of healing. The Sunday school kids would even come to my house and I reached out to those who needed help, who were struggling because of abuse and rejection and covered them in prayer. Sometimes instead of us having spiritual dancing or drama practice, they shared their problems and struggles and we prayed together. Some of the kids grew spiritually and God intervened in their home situations. I knew if I did what God wanted me to do then nothing was impossible for God. Sometimes I wonder where I would have been today if my mom had not fallen ill. I had always wanted to become a nurse. Everything had worked out so perfectly for me to become one. When I worked at Wentworth Spar, I had met a friend who was a nurse and she gave me all the information I needed including the application forms. I had applied to Albert Luthuli Hospital in Durban and then my mom got sick. I was afraid she was going to die while I was away training. I now realized God had allowed mom to get sick because His plan for me was to work with children and He had planned it from before I was born. He is God and He did what He had to do for me to live out my calling, which is Children's Ministry, and not nursing. Can you see how God works? We must remember that God will not anoint us for ministry that He has not ordained for us to do. If God is doing something crazy in your child's life and your hopes of your son/daughter becoming someone great is put on hold, know that God has something better in mind. We cannot choose what we want our kids to become in life if God has already chosen their profession or career. God knows the plan He has for them and it is always a better plan.

THE PURPOSE BEHIND THE PROBLEM

CHAPTER 12

Faith versus Fear

I returned from work and discovered someone had broken into the house. Most of our belongings, extension cords, clothes, music CDs and other items Iwere missing. I went to the police and opened a case. I later discovered that it was one of Cammy's friends. Cammy was nowhere to be found so I went in search of him. I walked, walked, and finally decided to try some of his friends. Most of them had not seen him and others sent me on a wild goose chase. When I was about to call it a day, I bumped into another friend who pointed me toward a small room. By this time, I was more frustrated than ever, I was tired and my feet ached.

I made my way to the room that was situated at the back of the main house and knocked on the door. The stale smell of dampness, sweat and urine greeted me when the door was flung open and I found myself looking into the eyes of eight youth. The atmosphere in the room became tense as they stared at me. I sensed that I had interrupted them; they were obviously in the middle of something. They wanted to know what I wanted as they looked me over from top to bottom and then one of them stood up and walked toward me very angry.

I mentioned that I was looking for Cammy and then it clicked to them who I was. The atmosphere immediately changed. "Oh that skraal laity, yes he used to hang out with us but then he joined some other friends, we going to show him for messing with us." The biggest one, a 23-

THE PURPOSE BEHIND THE PROBLEM

year-old, who was flicking a lighter and holding a cigarette came and stood beside me. I was suddenly gripped with fear and measured the distance from where I was standing to the door planning how to escape.
 Suddenly I felt a power within me arising and swallowing all my fear and I thought to myself, it's now or never. I remembered God's promise that He will never leave me nor forsake me and I suddenly realized that Jesus within me was greater than all boys who were trying to intimidate me.
"Please tell Cammy that I am looking for him." I tried to sound bold and stern. My eyes scanned the room and I observed that the other boys were much younger than the one standing beside me. Maybe he was their gang leader or the owner of the place. "Thanks, and sorry for intruding." They looked at me not knowing what to say but the atmosphere became tenser. "Look you don't have to do this, Jesus loves you. Maybe no one has told you that before but the Lord loves you." With those words, I turned and walked out the door unharmed.

On another occasion, while I was on my way to one of my Sunday school children's home in Tjoksville, a gangster snatched my cellphone out of my hand just as I was about to make a call. He tried to scare me off by picking up a brick and threatened to smash my face but I told him that I was a woman of God and that God would punish him for taking my phone. The surprised look on his face caused the brick to fall to the ground slowly and he handed back my phone with a very worried look on his face. He was once a child of God who had backslides two years ago. I told him that it was never too late to

THE PURPOSE BEHIND THE PROBLEM

come back to the Lord and as I left, I asked his name and told him I will bear him up in prayer. His friends could not believe what they saw. They were waiting to help him sell my phone but God was on my side that day. I walked away with a new confidence that day, thanking Jesus that He came to my rescue.

I had found out over the years that one of the devil's favorite devices was to try to intimidate us through fear. I had reached a stage where I was not prepared to compromise Jesus or the truth and Cammy's previous disappearance had often led me to tread on gangster territory where I had to stand my ground as a child of God. Returning home after this experience, I began to pray and the Lord reminded me of three important truths that I immediately recorded in my journal. God said I am *bigger*, I am *able* and I am *in control*.

Needless to say, it was not long before that threatening group helped me to find Cammy. With our great God on our side and His Mighty Holy Spirit within us, surely we have all we need to live lives where faith constantly triumphs over fear.

CHAPTER 13

Warning and Breakthrough

God took me from one spiritual level to another especially at the Joshua Project where I was in ministry and living out my calling. I really enjoyed working with the children and daily, God was busy at work in my life. As I grew in the Lord, He increased my love for the children and connected me with people from different lifestyles. My mission was still to find a place to stay. The time was drawing near for us to move out. It seemed that the same routine was happening every time. Whenever we moved into a new house and had it repaired and painted then we had to move out after a few months. We had started house hunting but there were no empty houses available. I had prayed and received no answer and the property owner constantly came to find out if we had found another place. There were absolutely no places but I knew that God never fails and that he will not disappoint us. He will make a way.

As I continued to fast and pray, I had a dream one night of a beautiful, big house with white walls inside. I knew that God had reserved a house for me somewhere. There were absolutely no places available but I knew God never fails and he will not disappoint us. He will make a way. My sister Rina and I, kept in contact and we decided if the Lord does not open another door, then we will know that our time in Jeffrey's Bay is up, that its

THE PURPOSE BEHIND THE PROBLEM

God will for us to go back home and if there's an open door then our time is not yet up.
A week later, the property owner showed up and again asked for our ID numbers. She said that Mr. Palmer could not find the documents she had given to him at the municipality offices. She then told us that we have another three months to find a place and I immediately knew this was the working of God. He had prolonged the time because He knew that there were no houses available. I was so grateful to God for stepping in.

I was surprised when Rina ended up in Jeffrey's Bay and ended up on my doorstep. This also served as confirmation that I was in Jeffrey's Bay to stay longer. The enemy just would not leave me alone and I was under attack almost every day. When I went to church, God spoke to me about a message that I had received through prophecy years ago and I realized that my breakthrough was near, that Satan was attacking me to distract me from my blessing. I knew that God knew that I had to be out of the house by the end of the month. Since that day I placed my faith in God and knew that He will not let me down, that He will come through for me at precisely the right time. That same week my sister and I went to look at a house in Whale Street but I felt it was not the place for me. When I prayed and asked the Lord to show me whether that was the house, He opened another door for a place in St Croix Street.

We went to see the house and I loved it but the rent was very high because it was in the industrial area. God then reminded me of the time I moved into my house with no

THE PURPOSE BEHIND THE PROBLEM

job, no money and no food. All I had was faith! This time I had more than that so I needn't doubt Him because He is able to do abundantly and gracefully much more than I can hope for as His word assures us in Romans 8:32 *he gave us His Son- will he not also freely give us all things?* Immediately all fear and doubt vanished as I realized my God is rich, he owns all the cattle on a thousand hills and He will come through for me financially.

A few days before we could move in, the person who had fixed the locks disappeared with the key and were nowhere to be found. Then I heard that the geyser was leaking so we could not move in. I was disappointed but then God made me understand that He was causing the delay for a reason. Even the landlord was reluctant to let us move in with a leaking geyser. All I did was pray. The present property owner was putting pressure on us to move out. I went on my knees and prayed. I had so much trust and confidence in God and knew He was busy with my situation. With God, delays are not denials and His timing is perfect. The fact is God is higher than a property owner or president of a country and if God has not given me the answer, then I have to wait. I cannot rush God or meddle where He is busy.

A few days later while spending time with God, the Lord told me that something was going to happen that would shatter me and breaks my heart.
I then had a dream of me being highly pregnant. I was wearing this beautiful floral pink maternity with small flower designs and I was on my way to the doctor. I was shocked when the doctor told me I was expecting twins

THE PURPOSE BEHIND THE PROBLEM

and he immediately saw by my expression that this was something that was unplanned and shocking. I told him that I did not want any more kids because I wanted to do the work that God had called me for and besides I wasn't supposing to bear any more kids after my operation. He then asked me what was I going to do with the kids and I knew that I had to make a decision before I gave birth. Suddenly my alarm went off, and I woke up.

A few days later at work, one of the team members said she had dreamt of babies and I remembered my dream. God gave me the answer. It appeared that it was not I who was pregnant; spiritually God was pregnant with a double portion of my blessing. Habakkuk 1:5 Look *at the nations and observe for I am going to do something in your days that you will not believe, even if you were told.*

THE PURPOSE BEHIND THE PROBLEM

CHAPTER 14

It Never Rains but Pours

I will never forget this day. It was about 7:10am when the owner of the house I was renting and her daughter stormed in. They demanded that we move out Iand even when we tried to explain what had happened to the house we were supposed to move into, they refused to understand. They argued and screamed and I knew I had to withdraw and go and pray while they argued with my husband. I began to call upon the Name of my Lord and Saviour to take control of the situation and open the door for us for another house. I even reminded God of the prophetic word, He had given for my life 'that I will never be a scorn to the nation'. When I came out of the room, the situation had become worse, my things were being carried out but I still trusted that God would do something, so I told them I believe God will come through for us, we just needed time. They refused to listen and just would not give us a chance. They argued and screamed and left my husband no choice but to call the police. The police arrived, we explained our situation, and we were given until 14:00pm to move out (about 5 hours)

I cried to the Lord to help us as the tears ran down my cheeks. We walked and walked but there were no places available. I prayed as I walked asking God to open a door for us. Three times, we ended up by a friend who

THE PURPOSE BEHIND THE PROBLEM

had promised us a place but he was not at home and nowhere to be found. We were tired and hungry. By the time we got back, there was already a van load of furniture and the people were moving in on top of us. My heart broke. Where was God? I had trusted Him so much to do something. No, this could not be happening. "Why are you allowing this God?"
Why was God not doing anything to help me? I was hurt and heart-broken. I was frustrated and angry as my husband suggested that we had no choice but to remove the rest of our stuff and pile it into the tiny shed in the backyard. The tears just came rolling down as I sought answers from the Lord…but nothing! Somehow, I had the feeling to go to my neighbor, Monica who lived across the road and she agreed that we could use her little room until we found a place. We moved all our valuables, clothing and smaller items, which we had packed, into boxes and black garbage bags. My tears could not stop flowing as I talked to God in my heart. I still believed He would do something that we need not stay in the small room.

It was getting dark. Somehow, I felt that the Lord had forsaken me and yet I had trusted Him so much. I had never felt so embarrassed and humiliated in my life. How can the Lord whom I trusted and believed in do this to me?
Even the house that I was supposed to move to in St Croix Street, I was so heart-broken when the property owner had given the house to one of his relatives. I knew that God had closed that door, that he did not want me to stay there and I had accepted it. That was a beautiful

THE PURPOSE BEHIND THE PROBLEM

house with built-in kitchen cupboards, a lounge and two bedrooms with a bath and a shower. Therefore, when God closed this door, I trusted Him and knew he would open an improved door for a house that will be more beautiful than that one. Now I have to live in a small room with all my stuff still in boxes because there is no space. The place is too small to fit our beds into so we sleep on the cold floor.

As I stood in the room that evening, the tears just rolled, I was shattered and heart broken. I had even told the people that threw us out that God will come through for us and now I felt like a fool. The worse thing was that the room was not very small, it leaked and that very same night it rained. I cried myself to sleep that night asking the Lord a thousand questions. I asked the Lord why He had given us a place that He knew was leaking when He is God and could have opened any other door for us. As I prayed, the rain stopped. The minute I started thanking God for stopping the rain, it came pouring down more than before. We had to put buckets and basins under every leak and that night I hardly slept at all. I felt like Job who had lost everything. My couches, beds and the rest of my furniture that was in the shed were drenched with rain as the shed was leaking as well.

The next morning, some of my colleagues who had heard what had happened, popped in to encourage and support me.
My sister and I walked in the soaking rain looking for a place but there were no places available. I went home very disappointed and that afternoon I once again asked

THE PURPOSE BEHIND THE PROBLEM

God for mercy, to open a door for a place to stay. Our stuff was in boxes and bags and every time we needed something, we had to move all the boxes and bags to get space. It rained that whole week so all our laundry was piled up as well. I had no choice but to go to work the next day and one of my colleagues reminded me of the word God had given for my situation in Habakkuk 1:5. I ran into my office and wept. I realized that God was at work in my situation. He knew what I was going through.

THE PURPOSE BEHIND THE PROBLEM

CHAPTER 15

Noah's Ark

I got up with swollen eyes from crying and being in prayer the night before. My sister slept over at my cousin's place so I was able to sit in her corner and pray. I poured my heart out to the Lord. I remember Job did this. I was honest and told God how I felt, how disappointed and broken I felt. I told God that I did not want to be so desperate that I lose all hope and trust in Him because that is what happens to so many people. As desperate as I was to get out of that small room, I knew that only God could help me now as practically every one in every street had told us there were no places available. I had to wait upon God; He could open any door. He knew where He wanted me to stay. Presently there was not one open door so I prayed for God to let His will be done. It was not easy for the six of us to be cramped up in one small, little room. Every day we had to move bags and boxes to make place to sleep. The place leaked and was very cold. We called our little room Noah's Ark.

One evening as we had devotion, my sister and my son, Cammy rededicated their lives to God. That night as we all held hands and prayed, my colleague's words rang in my ears "this test is not only for you but for your entire family so you must ask God what it is that He wants you all to do." That night I felt in my spirit that we had to forgive and release the people who had thrown us out, so

THE PURPOSE BEHIND THE PROBLEM

we forgave them and asked God to forgive them for causing us hurt and pain. That night I felt so relieved and as I fell asleep, God gave me a sign to show us that our breakthrough was near.

That night I dreamt I was in a room where pregnant women were walking in. They appeared to be in labor and were ready to give birth. They walked in one by one until there were seven of them and when the last woman walked in she went into labor. I looked at my stomach and realized I was not pregnant so I asked the Lord what I was doing among all these pregnant women. The answer was that I would pray for them but when I placed my hand on the lady that was in labor and was about to pray, the Holy Spirit told me that there is no need to pray, as her baby is on the way and about to be born. However, before I could see the baby I woke up. It must have been the early hours of the morning when I woke up and I felt such peace as I connected with God and I felt 'breakthrough'. God had already given birth to the answer for a house. A few hours later, my sister and I prayed and asked God to direct us to the house He wanted us to move to. At 5:00pm, we ended up outside a house in Roman Street but there were people staying in the house. Nevertheless, we explained our situation and they explained they were only looking after the place. They were relatives of the owners of the house. God just took over and they actually allowed us to sleep in the house that night without paying a cent. The next day the Lord made it possible for us to contact the property owner and once again, when the rent was too high, God

THE PURPOSE BEHIND THE PROBLEM

stepped in and made it possible for me to pay only R1 500.00. Praise God!

God told me to anoint the house and God just poured out His mighty anointing over the place. By two o' clock that afternoon, we had moved in. I thanked and praised God as I realized that this house was bigger and better than the previous one. The whole house was tiled, had three bedrooms with built-ins and an end suite, big lounge with a built-in room divider and the kitchen had built-in cupboards with a breakfast nook. When I personally met the owner at a later stage and she explained the story of the house, I could not hold back my tears. It appeared that a week before I could move into her house, some people had contacted her husband because they wanted to rent her house but her husband had refused and she said she could not understand why. When I had phoned, her husband had immediately agreed to me paying R1500.00 instead of the full rental amount. Shaeeda was a Muslim and could not understand the reason for my tears but when I sat her down and shared my testimony, she no doubt left knowing that Jesus was the reason that I became her tenant. God had a reason for us to meet so she could hear about the Man of Galilee who had changed our lives and our situation.

THE PURPOSE BEHIND THE PROBLEM

CHAPTER 16

Pain, Heartache and Tears to Release the Past

I stood at the open grave with a shattered heart as the pain ripped through my body, tears streaming down my cheeks. As the coffin was lowered, I closed my eyes and said a silent prayer to God knowing that I would never see Cameron again but also understanding that God knows best. I felt a tug on my arm as Enver put his arms around me trying to comfort me. Then I was forced to move forward to throw some rose petals as the coffin reached its resting place. This was the hardest thing I ever had to do in my entire life. I suddenly felt weak and silently asked the Lord to give me strength as I clutched my husband's arm and slowly moved forward.

After the funeral, I sat in my room and had a conversation with God as he reminded me of every detail leading up to my son's death. Cameron's sister, aunt, niece and cousins whom I had not seen for years, all came to bid him farewell. I remembered the day Cammy came home and told me he wants to recommit his life to Jesus and be delivered from being involved in drugs and crime. Fortunately, Prophet Ashley was holding prayer sessions at the church that day and I advised Cammy to attend. He came home with a glow on his face and I was so grateful to the Lord that he had been obedient. A week later, he was threatened by gang members and he had to leave Jeffreys Bay as he refused to be involved in

THE PURPOSE BEHIND THE PROBLEM

the former things. He got a job and worked in Hankey, returning after three weeks. I invited him to church the Sunday and he connected with Prophet Ashley again after church asking him to continue to pray for him. On 30 June 2018, he was attacked by a gang in Jeffreys Bay and they chopped him on his back and on his arm and damaged his elbow. He was in David Livingstone Hospital for a week and I prayed fervently for his safety when he returned.

On the 10 July 2018, God spoke to me saying He has seen my tears and heard my prayers for my family. He *will* save my husband and my son. He is going to do something to release me from my past because the thing from my past is holding me back. He is going to cause a mighty wind to blow away and take me into a new season. It is a season of new things even for my husband and my son.

Cameron promised me he would never go back to his old ways and left for Humansdorp on the day he was discharged. I phoned him to pick up his bandages and medication he had forgotten and on route to the taxi a few days later, he kept telling me he needs to go away and might not return. I asked him why and told him that God would protect him no matter what. He called me after a few days and I asked him when he was coming to visit but he replied "Mummy for how long?" and I could not understand why he had said that.

It was a Sunday evening service at Emmanuel Church and I was called to the front as Prophet Ashley began to

THE PURPOSE BEHIND THE PROBLEM

prophesy. He said two things will happen to Enver; the sore on his hand will dry up and be healed and the demon that is sent to suck his blood and life away will be gone. He said he sees me weeping in prayer for my family and God is going to bring peace and restoration between us. He further prophesied about my sons and mentioned Cameron who wanted to come home but… then he said that I was going to receive a phone call.

On Thursday night 9 August I had a dream of Cameron coming into the house so gracefully. He was smiling as he looked at me. It looked like he was dressed in white and seemed to be looking for his brother, Tyrell. I asked him when he was coming home and he replied that he will not ever be coming home. Before I could reply he was gone.
 On Saturday, 11 August, this was the worst day of my life. I got up feeling tired and cleaned up. I had planned to go to my neighbor, Ashwell father's funeral but then I just had the feeling that I need to stay at home. My tummy suddenly felt bloated so I went to the toilet but took my phone with me, something I rarely do. This was the time I received the phone call about Cameron's passing. Luckily I was sitting or I would have hit my head on the floor. Enver arrived just a few minutes before the police came and delivered the news which I had already received.

THE PURPOSE BEHIND THE PROBLEM

CHAPTER 17

Look at the Purpose not the Problem

Call unto me and I will answer and show you great and mighty things you do not know, Jeremiah 33:3. This is one of my favorite verses in the Bible. Circumstances, situations and problems sometimes have a way of weighing us down but God teaches us vital life lessons through our problems. We must remember that there is a reason for everything that happens to us.
The story about a beautiful, experienced dressed woman who complained to her psychiatrist that she felt that her whole life was empty, it had no meaning. Therefore, the woman went to visit a counselor to seek out happiness. The counselor called out the old woman who cleaned the office floors and then said to the rich woman "I am going to ask Mary here to tell you how she found happiness." Therefore, Mary put down her broom and told her story. "Well my husband left me for another woman; my mom died of cancer and three months later, my only son was killed by a car. I had nobody. I had nothing left. I could not sleep. I could not eat. I never smiled at anyone. I even thought of taking my own life. Then one evening, a little kitten followed me home. Somehow, I let the kitten in and gave it some milk. It licked the plate clean and rubbed itself against my leg and for the first time in months, I smiled. Then I stopped to think, if helping a little kitten could make me smile, maybe doing something for people could make me happy. Therefore,

THE PURPOSE BEHIND THE PROBLEM

the next day I baked some biscuits and took them to the neighbor who was sick in bed. Every day, I tried to do something nice for someone. Today I sleep like a baby. I have found happiness by giving it to others."
When she heard that, the rich woman cried. She had everything that money could buy but she had lost the things which money cannot buy. The beauty of life does not depend on how happy you are, but how happy others can be because of you. Happiness is not a destination; it is a journey. Happiness is what you *are* not what you *have*.

I do have a clearer and better understanding now of how God deals with us or our problems and most of the time, we do not see the problem through God's eyes. God gives us a tiny piece of the puzzle. Take e.g. the incident where I was put out of the house by the property owner. God did warn me that something was going to happen that would shatter me and break me, before I was put out of my house. He did warn me! He did prepare me! Even the death of my son was God's way of releasing me of my past because my ex-husband's family not only attended the funeral but we had a chance to make peace. This was what Prophet Ashley spoke about, that God would restore the family! I guess when we are in the situation we only see the problem and *not the purpose behind the problem.*
Whatever you are going through, whatever your situation is or whatever your challenges are right now, remember God loves you. He promised *that He would never leave you nor forsake you.* There is a purpose for what you are going through right now! Ships do not sink because of

THE PURPOSE BEHIND THE PROBLEM

the water around them. They sink because of the water that gets in them. It is the same with trouble; we cannot stop what is on the outside: opposition, offense, delays, criticism, hatred, politics, and favoritism. These things will come. The key is not to let what is on the outside, get on the inside. Shut the door to the enemy, cut out the chaos and confusion. When you experience hard times declare, "God, there is trouble all around me and it does not make sense but I am not letting it get to me or in me. I know that *no weapon formed against me shall prosper.* I know that *those who wait on the Lord shall renew their strength, they shall mount up with wings like eagles, and they shall run and not be weary. They shall walk and not faint."* (Isaiah 40:31) Doing things God's way brings about promotion and gets us ready for increase. Favor will follow your life as you follow and obey God.

Maybe you cannot see the purpose, all you see is your problem, which appears to be bigger than God is, but God knows all about your problem. God uses pain as a shaping tool for those He loves. One of the important things I have learnt is that we are part of God's pre-determined will so before anything even happens to us, God already knows. He knows how we would react if anything happens to us and around us. God knew how you would react when you lost your job, when your daughter fell pregnant and why, he knew your emotions when you lost your dad, mum or a sibling. God already knew. He knew how you would react when it happened and whatever happened after it had happened. God knows everything. It is not what happens to us that

THE PURPOSE BEHIND THE PROBLEM

matters, it is how we respond to what happens that makes the difference.

I could have given up on God, turned my back on him and called him a liar when I was put out of my house, but I did not. I remained faithful and trusted Him even though I was in a small, cold, leaking room, cramped up with all my stuff. I could have asked God a thousand questions while standing at my son's open grave and turned my back on Jesus but I did not. Sometimes we suffer not because we do wrong, but because the devil wants us to give up on God and turn our backs on Christianity. Sometimes God allows us to go through a problem to strengthen and equip us for future ministry or for our calling, but we sometimes only see the problem. Untold masses of believers lose hope, trust in God, and backslide because they are not aware of the enemy's evil devices and schemes; some even blame God.

From the beginning God knew exactly *how*, *when* and *where* you and I would encounter hurt and pain, disappointments, abuse and discouragements but He allows it to happen for a reason.

Job in the Bible was a righteous man who loved and feared God but he was afflicted. God uses affliction to teach us His word and to build our faith, so we end up closer to Him than we were before our troubles began. My faith in God has soared since my problems. Our troubles are not about us; they are about God. They are sent to teach us things about God we could not learn any other way. Martin Luther commented that he never learnt the word until he was afflicted, his sufferings were schoolrooms.

THE PURPOSE BEHIND THE PROBLEM

This is a harsh reality for many Christians to face because we do not like dealing with negative circumstances. When we bring God into the equation, we can look back and see it was good for us to go through hard times because we learnt truths about God and ourselves that we never have known. About God, we learn that His ways are far beyond our ways, that He is holy and Righteous and full of mercy and He is *always* faithful to His children. We always learn we are not as wise, as powerful, or as clever as we thought we were and in the end, we are exposed as helpless children desperately in need of our Heavenly Father.

Psalm 119:71 David says *it was good for me to be afflicted so that I might learn your decrees.* Therefore, David learnt something about himself and God during his time of affliction. Affliction comes in all shapes and sizes; a head cold, a major sickness, the loss of a job or a loved one, public persecution or rumors spread by our enemies. On the other hand, the affliction could be the type of suffering that Job experienced.
We must thank God for all our troubles (Thessalonians 5:18) There are always reasons for gratitude no matter how dim, how bleak or grim our circumstances may seem (imagine if God never made a way for us to be in that small room, we were going to sleep on the street)

If we look carefully how God has been at work bringing blessings through the troubles of life, we will see His fingerprints. Look for God's fingerprints in your life, look for evidence of answered prayer, the work of the Holy angels in your family's life and yours. Think about

THE PURPOSE BEHIND THE PROBLEM

this: if Joseph's brothers never threw him into a pit, sold him, lied to his father that he was dead; Joseph would never have ended up in Egypt as head of Potiphar's household and in charge of the entire land, property and overseer of all the slaves. Then he was tested when Potiphar's wife falsely accused him of rape and he was thrown into prison where he interprets the dreams of the baker and the cupbearer. Are you in the dungeon, God can still use you! Do not give up on God! Joseph went from prison to palace after he correctly interpreted Pharaoh's dream. Because of God's favor upon his life, he becomes the prime minister of Egypt and is later re-united with his family because of a famine. Can you see the purpose of the famine? His family was forced to go to Egypt where Joseph was. What is the famine in your life today? God has a purpose for whatever you are going through.

Many of us are still troubled, still seeking, still making little forward progress because we have not come to the end of ourselves. We arc still trying to give orders and interfering with God's work within us. We want to have it all and do it all and become upset when it does not happen, then we notice that God gave others characteristics that we do not have and we respond with envy, jealousy and self-pity instead of just surrendering to God. God often calls surrendered people to do battle on His behalf. The battle is always over our future.

Immerse yourself in God's word. Read it, pray over it, and cling to it. Recite God's promises back to Him. Let God's word be the foundation of your prayers. Determine to obey the word no matter what happens to

THE PURPOSE BEHIND THE PROBLEM

you or around you. You will emerge with a faith much stronger than before your troubles started.

Don't give up, don't give in, you must tell the Lord you will continue to believe in Him no matter what happens *'Though he slays me; yet will I trust him'* Job 13:15. Sometimes we will face things for which there will be no earthly explanation. In those moments we need to erect, a sign that says or reads 'Quiet, God at work' the greatest tragedy is to miss what God wants to teach us through our troubles.
 If God never closed the door to my job years ago, I would never have gone to Jeffreys Bay. If my son never ran away from home, I would never have been part of the ministry at the Joshua Project. God used the trouble and the pain that my son caused me years ago, to get my attention to change my direction from what I wanted to do, to what God had called me to do and that is Children's Ministry. If my first property owner had not thrown me out, I would never have been blessed with all the furniture I have today. Do you see the pattern? Do not allow the devil to remove your focus from our Heavenly Father and the good plans he has for you. Even in the biggest problem and in the worst situation, Jesus is still King. He is able to turn every negative circumstance around and take you from a zero to a hero.

God helps us in our time of trouble so we are equipped to help others in their time of trouble. Remember it is *how* we respond to our problems and situations that make the difference. So don't look at your problem; focus on the *purpose* behind the *problem*!

THE PURPOSE BEHIND THE PROBLEM

References

1. (Page 13) David Asscherick's is the co-founder of ARISE. David currently pastors the Kings Cliff Seventh-day Adventist church in Chinderah, New South Wales, Australia. He is the former pastor of the Troy Seventh-day Adventist Church in Troy, Michigan. In 2011, ARISE merged with Light Bearers and David became co-director of Light Bearers.[] He has been featured on 3ABN and Hope Channel and has been a regular presenter at the annual Generation of Youth for Christ conferences.

2. (Page 13) Open doors and closed doors by **PASTOR** E. A. **ADEBOYE**

3. Regarding predestination, **Ephesians 1:5** tells us that God "predestined us to adoption as sons by Jesus Christ to Himself." Speaking of Christ, verse 11 says, "In Him also we have obtained an inheritance, being predestined according to the purpose of Him who works all things according to the counsel of His will." **Romans 8:29-30** adds, "For whom He foreknew, He also predestined to be conformed to the image of His Son that He might be the firstborn among many brethren. Moreover, whom He predestined, these He also called; whom He called, these He also justified; and whom He justified, and these He also glorified."

4. (WITCHCRAFT THEORY AND PRACTICES: Identifying and breaking Demonic Curses: John Eckhardt
HISTORY OF WITCHCRAFT, DEMONOLOGY, and ASTROLOGY AND OTHERMYSTICAL PRACTISES:
Witchcraft theory: Ly de Angeles
Richard Cavendish
HEALING: John Eckhardt

THE PURPOSE BEHIND THE PROBLEM

All Scriptures quoted from 'the King James Bible and Amplified Version

INSPIRATIONAL QUOTES: Food for Daily Living, Food for Thought,
 The Word for Today

Acknowledgements

*To Chillidave Publishers team who made it possible for this book to be a success.
*To my wonderful husband, Enver and my son, Tyrell.
*To my Beautiful dearest friend (Becky Vaughan
*To my lovely friend (Geraldine) who encouraged me in publishing this book.
*To my beautiful sisters (Rita) and (Jenny Gilbert) who supported me with love and prayer
*To my fans and supporters thank you for being part of my writing journey.
*To Prophet Ashley, you have been my inspiration, many thanks to you for fervently praying for me.

THE PURPOSE BEHIND THE PROBLEM

THE PURPOSE BEHIND THE PROBLEM

For Bookings

Email: marghoskins@gmail.com
Publisher: Chillidavepublishers@gmail.com
Manager: Tlhomphodavid@gmail.com
Facebook Page: Margie Hoskins-Author
             Chillidave Publishers
Instagram: @Marg Hoskins
           @DavemTlhompho
Twitter: @Margie Hoskins Author
         @DavemTlhompho
Call: (074) 272 7044 / (087) 510 1435

THE PURPOSE BEHIND THE PROBLEM

THE PURPOSE BEHIND THE PROBLEM

Authors Profile

Margie Hoskins was born in KwaZulu-Natal and relocated in Pellsrus, Jeffrey's Bay in Eastern Cape. She is a Coordinator and Children's Minister as well as an Administrator at Emmanuel Assembly, A Teacher and Children's Church Training Conductor, Events coordinator and decorator for functions and weddings. She is a Motivational speaker, church Stewart, Social Entrepreneur, Author and Teacher. She has completed short courses in early childhood development; she is currently interested in Biblical Counseling for young adults and children.

Margie Hoskins is a community developer, motivational speaker and an Author of the Purpose behind the Problem.

She is currently busy with studies on Biblical Counseling for children.

There's no easing up for Margie Hoskins regardless of her tight schedule, as a foster mom, who goes extra miles helping everyone who needs her expertise.

She has formerly worked at an NPO working with vulnerable children and teaching spiritual dancing.

Margie Hoskins
Author |Motivational speaker |events planner| Life coach | Children's Counsel | Spiritual dancer | Innovative strategist compelling teacher and amazing community developer

THE PURPOSE BEHIND THE PROBLEM

www.ingramcontent.com/pod-product-compliance
Lightning Source LLC
Chambersburg PA
CBHW060206050426
42446CB00013B/3008